Out of the Habit

Finding Happiness, Meaning and Fulfillment Through A Life On Purpose

ANIKA J. GREEN

Contents

Introduction 1

Chapter One: A Life on Purpose 11

   You can't have it all 16

   What matters most? 22

   Making your own choices 25

Chapter Two: The Icarus Problem 31

   All-or-nothing thinking 37

   Taking action & finding balance 42

   The Law of Attraction 47

   The role of the brain 49

   What it means to take action 51

Chapter Three: How to Be an Enthusiast 55

   How to Become an Enthusiast 65

Chapter Four: Goals 83

   What is a successful goal? 84

   How to Hit Successful Goals 90

Chapter Five: Habits 105

   The importance of habits 107

   The Habit Loop 112

   Breaking the cycle 118

   Habits and who you want to be 123

Building healthy habits 125

Chapter Six: Know Yourself 133

Who you are 138

Self-sabotage: the unforeseen enemy 144

Boundaries 149

Chapter Seven: Intentional Healing 159

Trauma-based mindsets 164

Chapter Eight: Community 167

The Chameleon Effect 173

How to find your people 175

How to build intentional community 181

Chapter Nine: A Love on Purpose 191

Relationship Myths 197

How to love on purpose 205

Chapter Ten: Like There's No Tomorrow 215

A Note From the Author 223

Acknowledgments 227

References 229

Resource Page 235

About the Author 239

Introduction

don't believe in the pursuit of happiness.
It's a nice idea, don't get me wrong—the pot of gold at the end of the rainbow. For a lot of people, searching for happiness is synonymous with living. It's the human condition—what we're here to do. Our sense of purpose, satisfaction, and success in life are often driven by a desire to be happy.

Plastered on billboards, exploding on social media, and tattooed on people's bodies are phrases like "Choose your own happiness above all else", and "Cut out anything that doesn't serve you." Our brains are constantly bombarded by a narrative that tells us not just to pursue happiness, but to elevate and idolize it. To see all life as the means to that end.

I disagree.

Did you know that most of your happiness is actually genetic?

According to Harvard Medical School,[1] 50% of your potential happiness is based on biological factors determined at birth. 10% is determined by your circumstances. The remaining 40%, however, is decided by the choices that you make.

It's at this point that we usually mess it all up. First, we tend to drastically overestimate that self-inflicted component. 40% is less than half. Most of your happiness is not up to you at all. A majority of it is out of your control before you even *begin* to look at what's going on in your life. The idea that happiness is a light switch you can flip is just false.

But that's not all. Perhaps even more dangerous is what we choose to do with this information. One thing that we can all agree on is that because that 40% is all that we can affect, what we do with it really, really matters.

Our tendency is to jump to the conclusion that if our happiness is determined by our choices, all we need to do is make choices that make us happy.

Except that it's not quite that simple.

Every time you make a choice in life, you are at the same time *not* choosing your other options. By picking up this book, you chose not to read something else. When you do the dishes in the evening, you choose not to have a messy kitchen. Committing to a monogamous relationship means electing not to have other partners.

Every choice that you make has consequences, if only that it means you are not choosing something else.

The problem with adopting the pursuit of happiness as a mindset is that it keeps your vision pretty limited. You look at each choice as a separate decision rather than as part of a whole. They are one-offs, flukes, or simply snapshots of a much bigger picture. These little choices we make seem insignificant in the moment, but over time, they compound, combine, and create an entire life.

It's much more accurate to think of these everyday choices as bricks. It is an undeniable truth that with every second, hour, and day of your life, you are building *something*. Those small choices become habits, a one-time decision becomes a regular one, and one way or another, you lay the foundation for the future of what your life—and happiness—will look like.

The Happiness Problem

It's here that the pursuit of happiness as a way of life becomes problematic. Many of life's greatest joys aren't achieved through one-step choices, in fact, the majority of them take time and effort. It's not always blood, sweat, and tears, but it's also not always fun.

Strong relationships only stay strong when you learn how to work through conflict. Landing your dream job may require you to spend a few years in unsatisfying positions to gain experience. Staying healthy and active, a crucial contributor to personal happiness, frequently requires sacrifice of both physical energy and time.

It's not that wanting to be happy is a problem—it's a natural, inevitable part of being human. But when happiness starts to become isolated as the be-all, end-all, ultimate goal in your life, you're likely to end up feeling just the opposite.

Happiness is great. But it's not everything, particularly when the happiness you're chasing is a series of short-lived highs.

In fact, I have a theory that what we crave isn't actually happiness at all. That what we're searching for isn't a good mood, laugh, or temporary high.

I think if we are really honest with ourselves, what we want is purpose.

A sense of meaning and value in the world. A reason to get up in the morning that's bigger than just existing. Goals that are greater than a 401k and a paid-off mortgage.

We want to feel alive. Important. To wake up and actually contribute something to the world and each other and go to bed content and happy to wake up the next day and do it all over again.

For a long time, I thought that this kind of life was fictitious and unattainable.

Spoiler alert—it's not. And I am living proof.

I can't remember a time in my life when I didn't long for something more. As a kid, I used to dream up different worlds and lives and adventures for myself, longing for meaning and excitement in what I considered to be a very mundane existence for a seven-year-old. By age twelve, I was researching apartments in Los Angeles and New York City, desperate for a greater and more glamorous existence than my small Western Canada hometown could offer.

At the time, I believed that in order to live passionately and purposefully, I had to do things that shook the world. To see and do everything, to carve a new path, to go where no man had gone before, and live big and boldly and unexpectedly.

And so, at seventeen, I moved to the city—Vancouver, not New York—and pursued just that. But despite the increased opportunity around me and the excitement I expected to find, I was *absolutely miserable*. I'll get more into my story later, but for now, I'll tell you that I had, for years, believed that life was only worth living when it was loud or different or Insta-worthy.

We live in an over-saturated world that is constantly pushing us to look for more. More money, more stuff, more success—and yet, none of it brings lasting peace or contentment.

We may not actively confirm these messages, but the reality is that we are constantly being influenced by the world around us. The spaces we walk into have an effect on who we are. The human brain is an ever-absorbing sponge, taking in information, ideas, and messages we don't even realize we're being sent.

You may have an idea of what matters to you, where you want to end up, and who you hope to become—but what are you doing about it?

It doesn't matter how much willpower you have, how many TED talks you watched this week, or whether Mercury is retrograding today—if you're not consciously shaping yourself, the space you're in will do it for you.

The world around us isn't neutral. For better or worse, we are always being made into something. That's not a process you can turn off or opt-out of—but it is something you can leverage.

I have found that real happiness, passion and purpose are rarely caused by your circumstance.

Life doesn't need to be bursting at the seams in order to be full. By identifying what matters most to me, practicing intentional living, and pursuing purposeful habits and relationships, I'm actually living a life that I *love* waking up to every day. It's not the glamour I dreamed of—it's *so* much better than that.

This book outlines a different way to live.

A better way.

A chance to find fulfillment and meaning in every second.

Living on purpose puts the things that matter most at the center of your life. It helps you pursue what you love and stop wasting time on the things that don't matter.

This perspective will revolutionize your relationships, mindset, and understanding of happiness. Whether you want to see the world, be a killer stay-at-home mom, crush cases in the courtroom, run your own business, or all of the above—if you have big goals, passion, and a desire for purpose, this book is for you.

The *last* thing I want to do is write a cheesy self-help book promising you the answers to all your problems—let me cut to the chase, I don't have them.

I don't know your individual circumstances or struggles, and I respect you too much to pretend that life is that simple.

I have been living on purpose for years now, and it hasn't kept me from the human experience. Grief, anxiety, and hurt still have a place in my life. I still make mistakes, sometimes wake up in a crappy mood, and become dangerous to be around when I'm not caffeinated.

Intentionality won't keep you from the inevitable

pains of life. But what it will do is give you the tools to keep living well in spite of them.

I am so, so excited to get this into your hands.

Before we start, there are a few things that you should know—some key pieces of my own perspective and worldview that will play a part in this book. I understand that pure objectivity is impossible, and with that in mind, I want to be fully clear about where I'm coming from before getting started:

1. I believe you are here for a reason. That your existence on this earth is no accident, and that you have inherent value and potential that you cannot lose.
2. I believe that at our core, each one of us was born with a built-in need for purpose.
3. I do not believe that there is a cookie-cutter "right" way to do life. Each of us has different gifts, desires, and needs, and a purposeful life looks different for everyone.
4. My sincere hope is not that this book leaves you feeling warm and fuzzy—but that you are actually moved to act. To make impactful change, do things differently, and walk away with a greater understanding of who you are.
5. I'd like to note that not all concepts, ideas, or stories in this book are the product of my own 1. I have spent the last several years studying, implementing, and benefitting immensely from the research of others. In the back of the book, I've included a resource page with books, talks,

articles, and podcasts that have all impacted my growth in significant ways. Many of them are a more detailed look at some of the concepts in this book. I can't recommend them enough.

This way of living has changed everything for me. It's my deepest hope that this book leaves you lit up— uncommonly inspired, excited, and enthusiastic in the little moments.

Whatever your background, situation, or goals—we all get one life. It's worth doing well.

This is how to live on purpose.

CHAPTER ONE:
A Life on Purpose

What is Intentional Living?

t's no secret that we live in a world that loves to consume.
Seemingly from infancy, we are surrounded by a global media narrative telling us that we need to buy more, do more, and be more. Right out of the gate, we're meant to feel dissatisfied with ourselves and our lives.

Our priorities, desires, and actions are profoundly shaped by our surroundings. So much so, that without actively combating this influence, we can enter adulthood having never really made up our own minds.

There's no Merriam-Webster definition for the term "intentional living," but I like to think of it as living the opposite way—defining your own standards, expectations, and goals for life and going all in.

To put it simply, intentional living is a lifestyle of

purposeful action based around a clear goal, idea, or list of priorities.

Putting into practice the priorities you already think you have.

If someone asked you right now what mattered to you in life, you'd probably be able to answer pretty quickly. Most of us have at least some concept of what's important, be it family, faith, or influence. Our answers may vary, but we all have them.

The thing is, though—those priorities aren't always reflected in our lives. In fact, when we don't consciously keep them at the center of what we do, they almost never are.

Before I was introduced to the idea of living on purpose, I was confident that this was not the case for me. I made "good" decisions. I checked off my to-do lists. I tried to be a good friend. I used a daily planner, was working as a freelance writer, and had long-term goals I knew I wanted to hit.

To clarify, none of those are bad things at all—they were actually really good things. The problem for me was less what I was doing, and more that I'd never questioned why I was doing it.

I would classify that time in my life as "habitual existence" and nothing more. Maybe that's harsh, but the contrast to where I am now is so strong that it's hard to see it any other way. My days were the same, one after the other. Not meaningless by any stretch, but not meaningful, either.

I wasn't unhappy, but I also didn't really enjoy life all that much. There were highlights and exceptions, but the days were just... there.

It was normal. Underwhelming. Insignificant.

And while I intend no blame in this, it's what I was taught to expect. What we all were—grow up, get a job, save for a house, save for retirement, go on vacation once a year. You do it, because it's what you're supposed to do.

Once again, none of these things are negative. But a life built simply out of habit is likely not the one you want to live.

There's this thing we talk about in the Christian faith, that, even if you don't share the worldview, is relevant and important to this lifestyle. Essentially, the principle is that humans were created as worshippers. It's our instinct. We are always following, praising, glorifying and becoming *something*.

Sometimes that's other people, other times it could be career success, the desire for a relationship, financial stability, fame, wealth... Even personal growth can become an unhealthy idol in your life.

Whatever it is, *something* is making and shaping you—whether you know it or not. You are being influenced, and without conscious, intentional action, you may end up somewhere you didn't even realize you were heading.

Author Richie Norton once called intentional living "the art of making our own choices before others' choices make us"[1].

Intentional living is proactive. It doesn't ignore or undo the psychological realities of our humanness, but it puts you back in the navigator's seat. It opens your eyes to how the little things turn into big ones and it empowers you to take ownership of every area of your life.

Instead of unconsciously building a "normal" based on what's around you, this lifestyle will challenge and push you towards the things that mean the most to you.

The idea of purposefully, actionably living according to your own standards is just starting to become a conversation. Where pop culture's self-help gurus give you ways to take little breaks from life, intentional living creates a life you don't need a break from. When hustle culture tells you "Just keep pushing," intentional living asks why you're there in the first place, what you're giving up to be there— and if it's even where you want to be.

There isn't an objective "right" way to live (despite what your parents' disappointed faces may tell you)—but there is a wrong way, and it's going your whole life without ever even committing to the things you really love.

In this chapter, we're going to get to the root of what matters to you. Not just what you're used to or comfortable with—but the values, relationships, and dreams that are central to your life and heart.

As you go through this process, it's natural for a certain hierarchy to develop—different priorities carry different weights, and that's okay. Actually, it's really, really important to understand. I'd recommend grabbing a notebook or some of our free downloadable worksheets at *outofthehabit.com/downloads* to use throughout the book. Keeping a written record of your thoughts, notes, and the way that these priorities emerge and shift can be an extremely powerful way to process, and a great resource to look back on.

Your worldview comes into play here, too. I'm a Christian, and as a follower of Jesus, my priorities, relationships, and values are fundamentally shaped by the Word of God. Everything I believe about myself, other people, my time, my money, and my work is rooted here. My faith defines my core identity and priorities. My choices are shaped by this foundational part of who I am.

You don't need to share that to apply intentional living to your life. That's part of the beauty of it, and why this conversation is so very important.

At face value, this book has little or nothing to do with

your beliefs about the world, morality, humanity, and God—but in its application, these things are crucial. Intentional living is all about what matters to you. You could just as easily swap out "intentional" with authentic, honest, or conscious—and really, the lifestyle includes all of them and more.

A big part of this journey is simply getting to know yourself. Being honest with *you* so that you can be more honest with others and with the parts of your life that are not yet your own.

You can't have it all

Intentional living is often associated with living a minimalist lifestyle, and for good reason. The two ideas share a main principle that, while it may play out differently for some, is central to living a full life:

You can't have it all.

Or at least, you shouldn't—and trying won't do you any favours. I'm not a minimalist myself (yet), and I'm not going to go off about cleaning out your closet, even though we could all probably benefit from it.

Our consumer culture doesn't just infiltrate our homes and closets. Our minds, relationships, and schedules are almost constantly over-filled, so much so that when the world shut down in 2020, and we were forced to stay home, it brought with it a sense of *relief* for many.

Psychologist Carl Jung once described hurry as "not *of* the devil," but the devil itself. Our lives are full, too full, and we spend far too much time running around with energy levels that resemble an overdrawn bank account. We are in the negative, and still we add more - to our schedule, our list of emotional duties, and yes, our stuff.

Minimalism is often misunderstood as ridding your life of things you love or enjoy. If you don't *need* it, you should get rid of it. But this isn't true. In fact, the point isn't to get rid of anything—it's to create space for the things you DO love by eliminating the ones you don't. Think of it like pulling an extra tooth. When it's in there, all it does is take up room. Your mouth is cramped, probably painful, and it doesn't help you chew or speak more effectively. Pulling it simply makes it easier and more enjoyable to use the teeth you already have for their assigned purpose.

Weird metaphor, I know, but stick with me. The foundation of this whole process is knowing what you value. What you want to nurture, invest in, and maintain. The exercise that follows will help you identify what you most want to prioritize.

This is not a Buzzfeed quiz telling you what spice girl you are, but an exercise that's at the core of what it means to live intentionally.

This step will allow you to determine both where you are right now in your life and where you want to be. As you go through these questions, take the time to reflect and be honest with yourself about the things that hold meaning for you. These answers are for you alone.

Where are you now?

1. What are your priorities in life? Write down the top five and rank them according to their level of importance.

Knowing that you can't do it all, what core priorities do you want to protect? Family, career, personal growth, health, spiritual growth, travel, being a good parent, encouraging other people, being financially stable, fighting for justice, etc.

2. What do you spend your free time doing?

Is it working out, reading, writing, spending time with friends or family, working on a side hustle, getting sucked into the vortex of Instagram reels (hi, that's me).

3. What is the purpose of your job and how do you feel about it?

While it's true that your work life has no effect on your value as a person, it is impossible not to absorb our careers, at least in part, into our identity. What do you do all day and why? What are you doing it FOR? Is your paycheck the key motivator, or is there more to it?

4. How would your friends and family describe you?

Loyal, kind, consistent, busy, stressed, anxious, loving, generous... If you don't know the answer to this one, ask them. Shoot a message to a friend or family member and ask them to honestly describe you in 10 words or less.

5. How do strangers perceive you?

If you met you, with no context or information about who you are, what would you think?

6. What do you spend money on?

Pull out your most recent credit card or bank statement and look over your purchases. Reviewing what you actually spend money on can be a harsh reality check, but it's one of the most effective ways to see if your current lifestyle actually lines up with your priorities.

7. What does success mean to you?

What do you need to accomplish or collect in life in order to feel successful? What does "making it" look like and why?

8. What relationships matter the most to you and why?

Who could you not imagine living without? Who makes you who you are? Who is most important to you to see regularly? What about these relationships stands out, and why are they different from others?

9. What relationships matter the least to you and why?

On the flip side, what relationships are you a part of simply because it would be awkward to leave? Whose company do you value less and less?

Where do you want to be?

Use these next questions to think honestly about the kind of life that you want to live. This is your vision casting—it's time to dream up an ideal. Get as specific as you want, and don't limit yourself. Honesty is more important than "being realistic" for this exercise, so don't take something out or avoid writing it down because it feels big and impossible.

It's really easy to fall in love with the idea of someone else's life. Their social media feed, Pinterest boards, and highlight reels look picture perfect. Even their problems don't seem so bad. But this is your chance to fall in love with what *your* life could be. To play out the best case scenario and see where it could lead you.

1. Where do you want to be in 5 years?

Will you be prepping for parenting, getting ready for retirement, looking at colleges? Do you want to be at the height of your career? Do you even want to be in the same job or industry? What accomplishments do you expect to have in the next half-decade?

2. Where do you want to be in 20 years?

Play out the story a little bit longer—what's down the road from those 5 years? Are you picturing yourself in a thriving relationship, promoted to CEO, living in a little villa on the Amalfi coast? Maybe your goal is to stay right where you are—to simply create a better version of your life right now—invest more in your relationships, develop new skills in the workplace, build a healthier lifestyle.

3. What do you want to be known for by the people you are close to?

I like to ask myself the question "What would people say about me at my funeral?" It sounds grim, but it makes you think—how do I actually want to affect the people around me? What legacy do you want to leave for your loved ones and how do you want them to feel?

4. How do you want to impact strangers?

You can't be all things to all people, which is why the distinction between this question and the last is so important. How do you want to be perceived by people who aren't in your inner circle?

5. What goals are most important to you in life?

To put this another way, what goals of yours would be most devastating not to accomplish? What lifelong dreams are so deep in your soul that you would feel crushed by their absence?

6. If money was no object, what would you do for work?

Are there hobbies or interests that bring you joy? Passions you haven't explored?

What matters most?

A clear understanding of what matters most to you will shift over time. Through different seasons, your priorities will change, and in implementing intentional living, you may even realize that some things were more or less important than you originally thought.

None of your priorities or goals are locked in. As you change, so will your life, and so should it. This exercise is not to hold you down or cement what your life looks like, but to create a sense of direction, because before we get into the *how* of intentional living, you need to know your *why*.

There can be no purposeful action without first having some kind of purpose.

You can find a sense of purpose and meaning in a lot of ways, but this process can initiate a new way of thinking about your life and where you want to go. We are, however, going to take this one step further, because **a life on purpose doesn't just ask what matters, but what matters *most*.**

Look over your answers from the questions, and identify any common threads or overarching themes. Create a list of 3-5 permanent, long-term priorities. These aren't goals that can be achieved or items that could be put on a to-do list, but lifelong practices and habits that are always shaping you. They don't contradict each other and generally speaking, have some kind of compatible nature. These are the foundational pieces of the life you want to build.

They're the things that you will be constantly pursuing, growing in, and developing as a person. It's not hitting a certain promotion or moving to a specific city, but rather values like mental and physical health, quality relationships, integrity or spiritual life & relationship with God. These things become your core values, and they serve as a navigational tool for figuring out how to do life well.

All other decisions—what jobs to take, where to move, who to marry, how to spend your money—get held up to your core values. If something goes against these fundamental values and the very nature of the person you want to be, it's probably not for you.

Having a solid understanding of what this looks like in your life is so important. You are more than your decisions, and certainly more than your mistakes, **but a lot of your circumstances are the product of them**. Finding yourself in situations where you are living or acting in a way that contradicts these central parts of who you want to be can be devastating.

At one point or another, we've all been there—caught in a conversation we don't want to be a part of, stuck in a work environment that doesn't quite feel ethical, put in a position where we feel we have no choice but to violate our internal moral compass.

It's an awful, awful feeling. "To err is human"—and also inevitable—but we can minimize self-inflicted damage and pain in life simply by knowing and sticking by whatever hard and fasts are true for us.

The exclusivity of choice will force you to sacrifice some things, but if you are sure of what it is that matters most, it will never end up on the chopping block.

On the other hand, without a clear understanding of what you value most, you'll likely find yourself giving up things that you were never meant to. Sacrificing the best and most important for a little bit of everything never ends well.

Not everything is black and white, and sometimes you have to go into things blind, or get caught off guard by unforeseen outcomes. The goal here is not to escape the inescapable, but to be so confident in your identity and values that you are equipped to handle them when they come.

These 3-5 core values are your most matter-ful ones. These are the ones you write on your heart, the ones that anyone who knows you can see in you, and they really do make up the compass for where you are going. They are the foundational pieces of a purposeful life.

Making your own choices

Did you know that somewhere between 40-95% of your everyday behaviour is pure habit[1]?!

That's not a theory or a reprimand—it's a fact. Your brain craves repetition, and it is constantly looking for behaviours that it can make automatic. Think about how many choices you make without even thinking—driving a car, turning on the lights, picking up your phone.

If you scroll on any social media platform where

mental health and self-care are topics of discussion, you'll likely stumble across some tutorials on creating a kind of routine. Morning routines, skincare routines, there's how-to's on anything and everything. But I'm willing to bet that most people consuming that content don't realize that they already *have* routines. Whether you know it or not, your brain is repeating everything you do.

Being a person of routine is not a personality trait or quirk—it's literally how the brain functions. You are already living in a series of repeated actions. If you're anything like me, this information might make you start overanalyzing and assessing all of your everyday behaviours to try and find the patterns, followed by a little panic. But don't freak out—this isn't a bad thing. In fact, it's an unbelievably powerful opportunity.

Most of what you do is done without you even thinking about it. There's no self-help conference, motivational speech, or amount of inspiration that can change that. It's the way you're wired. We'll talk more about why in Chapter 4, and once you understand it, it can make everything you want to work towards so, so much easier.

Right now, what you need to understand is this:

If you are not consciously building your habits, they are unconsciously building you.

Your brain is not working against you. It's on your side, and habits themselves are a neutral tool that can be used either for your benefit or your detriment. Understanding how important this is is the first step (and in my opinion, easiest approach) to making lasting change in your life

This habitual part of our nature actually inspired the name of my blog and writing business, *Out of the Habit*. I'm a big fan of habits, but that phrase and name became a commitment to myself that no matter what, I would continue to live and write with intention and an awareness of what was going on around me. That I would not just be a product of the influence to which I was exposed, but rather a conscious force and contributor to the world and the things I believe in.

It's *this* that has brought me to where I am in life, and as you may be able to guess by the title, it's this that led me to write the book you're reading now.

Intentional living isn't about perfection. It's not about the show, getting a win, or "living your best life"—although I'd actually argue that the latter is a byproduct.

This is your life—and you only get one. So the way you live it matters.

Every day we live is made up of choices. From the little, seemingly insignificant decisions, to the world-changing, earth-shattering, life-defining moments, we are marked and moved by how we choose to live.

Knowing what matters to you is a *huge* step - it's the ground on which everything else is built. The goal now is to focus on creating a sustainable, intentional, powerful life, whatever that looks like for you.

As with anything, there will be highs and lows. Intentionality looks like rest days and quality relationships, but it also means setting boundaries and learning to walk away from *good* things that just aren't the *right* things.

Becoming the person you want to be requires you to let go of some parts of the person you have been. Letting old habits fall away and creating space for new rhythms.

A life on purpose is not for the faint of heart.

But it is for you—

the dreamer,

the passionate,

the one sick of waking up in the morning just to count down the hours until they can get back in bed.

The lost, the eager, the hungry. It's for you who crave happiness, who long for a sense of meaning in the mundane, for anyone and everyone who's ever wanted *more*—

It's out there. It's available. You are not stuck wherever you are. Whether your circumstances are wearing you down or you're realizing that the things that were supposed to fulfill you are just not doing the trick, a life on purpose can transform both where you are and how it feels.

Whether you know it or not, you are and have always been a person of purpose. You were created with intent, there is meaning in your story, and as long as you are breathing, it's not over yet.

Intentional living isn't the answer to the search for happiness. It's not a life hack, a teaser, or a self-care secret. But it is a better way of being, and that holds true no matter what your ideal looks like.

A life on purpose can't happen by accident. By its very nature, it has to be chosen—so I challenge you, wherever you're at, to do just that. To *choose* those things that matter most. To go all-in on what you love, and to dedicate your life and breath to something bigger and more powerful than happiness. To strive to be better, not because you're not good enough now, but because you're capable of more.

CHAPTER TWO:
The Icarus Problem

There's this story in Greek mythology about a boy named Icarus.

Icarus and his father Daedalus, an inventor, were imprisoned on the island of Crete. Hoping to escape, Daedalus built two pairs of wings out of feathers and wax for himself and his son. It was their only shot at freedom.

Before they took flight, Daedalus warned Icarus of the risk they faced. Their path needed to be direct. If they flew too low, the wings would become wet and heavy from the ocean spray. If they flew too high, the wax holding the wings together would melt.

Honestly, it wasn't *that* complicated—but what child do you know who, when given the chance to literally *fly*, would be focused on staying obedient to the advice of their protective parents?

Foolishly, and predictably, Icarus flew too high. Too close to the sun, his wings melted, and he fell to his own death.

While people have drawn many morals and conclusions from this tragic tale, the most common understanding is that ambition is what cost Icarus his life. His aspirations were too great, too high, to the detriment of his very existence. He was focused more on "living his best life" than staying safe. The story is a cautionary one, encouraging listeners to be wary of aiming too high.

It sends the message that risk is not worth taking. That dreaming too big leads to disappointment at best and tragedy at worst, and while the story is unique, the message is not.

Whether it's the critical voice of a parent telling you your childhood goals are unrealistic, a teacher discouraging you from chasing your passion, advice from well-meaning friends, colleagues who can't mind their own business, or simply your own internalized dialogue—the discouragement of ambition usually begins before we even hit puberty.

Rather than being normalized, failure becomes the ultimate enemy, and too often, we start to see ambition as its cause.

Of course, this is not *always* the case, but an unhealthy relationship to failure can be detrimental.

Our perception of success and failure, particularly at a foundational level, is largely determined by the people around us in our childhood. The first experiences we have with these ideas have a lot of impact on our lifelong relationships to the two.

There are a couple of very common mindsets that develop around these topics, and while I'm sure that there are some technical terms for them, I'm going to refer to them in the way that I understand them - the *Icarus* and the *Barbie Girl.*

1. The Barbie Girl

When I was growing up, there was this commercial that was *always* on TV. I haven't been able to get the song out of my head since. Every time it played, it displayed a different "career Barbie," each one followed by a little tune and the words "*I can do anything, I'm a Barbie Girl!*" (Mattel™)

It's sweet, right? Everyone likes to tell kids that they can have the world. This is one way that people respond to ambition. "You can do anything!" "You've got this!" "You're amazing!" It's encouragement, and it feels good.

And there's a healthy element to it—encouraging confidence, particularly in children, is important. But a lot of the time, it goes too far. Think of the kid on the TV talent show—the one whose parents have told him for his whole life that he has the voice of an angel. He's confident, right? Sure of himself.

And then he opens his mouth, and there's a collective cringe around the entire room. Not only has this child been lied to for his entire life, he's now in a position of intense vulnerability. Not just failing, but failing in front of the entire world.

There's a difference between encouraging someone to try and promising them success, and it's a really, really big one.

"You can do this!" is different from "You're the *best*!" False hope and empty encouragement are not helpful. Not only are they dishonest, they pose a serious and real threat to the healthy development of self-esteem.

In a bitterly ironic end result, they often reinforce the idea that an individual's worth is based on a talent or skill, which, once things don't pan out, can end up in a full-blown identity crisis.

Growing up, I was heavily involved in local theatre. In the area I was raised, competitive performance is a big deal. I was never athletic, a solid average in academics and music, but when it came to acting - that was my *thing*. I spent hours rehearsing, memorizing, and perfecting my pieces all year round.

I travelled to provincial competitions, completed exams with the Royal Conservatory, and fell in love with the world of drama. I started when I was 3, and continued every year (save one) until I graduated high school.

The last year that I competed, things were different. I was taking things more seriously, considering pursuing acting as a career. As I prepped for competition and my exam, I got a lot of affirmation.

Well-intentioned messages, comments, and lines flooded my ears—"This is your best year yet." "You've got this in this bag." "I've never seen anyone this good."

If it sounds like I'm getting cocky, just know that whatever pride I took from this came before a *very* hard fall.

After travelling to the provincial competition, not only did I not win, I didn't even place, something that had never happened to me at that level of competition. And it happened at the moment I was most sure of myself.

In my exam, the adjudicator—whose feedback is intended to be saved for comments read later—told me to my face that she actively disliked my performance.

And the teacher who had spent the year building me up and telling me how confident she was in what I would accomplish suddenly disappeared from my life.

And I was crushed.

It was a blow to my ego, but more than that, it destroyed the person that I thought I was. Putting so much of my identity into winning and accomplishing success in that area left me with nothing when it all fell apart.

No one meant to hurt me—I know that. And my self-created identity is my own responsibility. But this mindset had created such a tangible false reality for me that picking up the pieces took a few years.

The *Barbie Girl* mindset creates a fear of failure by prioritizing winning, success, and achievement—even when it doesn't mean to. It creates or confirms the idea that you *should* be where you want to be, and if you're not, there must be something wrong with you.

It breeds competition and almost always leads to an unhealthy view of your self-worth. On its own, this is bad enough—but it can actually flow right into the *Icarus* mindset as well.

2. The Icarus

The Icarus Mindset has the opposite problem and the same result. Instead of emphasizing winning or success above all else—instead of telling you that you're the best, you can do anything, or that failure shouldn't even be in your vocabulary, the Icarus mindset comes along and tells you to play it safe.

Rather than overvaluing achievement, this way of thinking prioritizes comfort, safety, and self-preservation. It is literally the act of letting the fear of striking out keep you from playing the game, but it goes back a few steps.

This mindset doesn't just tell you not to go after the things you want—it often tells you not to want them at all. This can look like an emphasis on setting realistic goals, studying something you're not interested in because it's a more reliable career, or staying in a relationship that's *fine* instead of waiting for one that's great.

Taking a gamble and leaping into the unknown is not something attractive to an Icarus Mindset. The risk of ambition and the consequences of leaping far outweigh the potential benefit of it. You stop before starting, give up rather than jump into the unknown without a harness.

Both these ways of thinking paint failure, and eventually ambition, as negative. Even the Barbie Girl mentality leaves you afraid to dream after one big loss. They can show up differently, but one way or another, both mindsets lead directly to all or nothing thinking.

All-or-nothing thinking

All-or-nothing thinking is exactly what it sounds like. The idea that in order to work towards something, you've got to give it all of you, 24/7, or there's no point. It's flying straight into the sun or never getting off the ground.

All-or-nothing thinking is perfectionism, a fear of failure, and procrastination wrapped up into one.

This thought pattern is embedded into so many of our minds via self-help books, inspirational quotes, and a culture that worships giving your all. "If you want it bad enough, you'll make it happen" came up on my Pinterest this morning.

Disguised as encouragement, the all-or-nothing mindset reinforces this false sense of self—that your confidence, self-worth, and pride must rest solely on your accomplishments. If this were true, it's no wonder that the threat of losing them would be so devastating. Why would you take any risk at all?

All-or-nothing thinking can look like:

- Refusing to try something that you don't think you'll succeed at
- Spending weeks, months, even years researching something before you dip your toe in (if you ever do)
- Only participating in activities you're already good at
- "I'm only as good as my last _____."
- Setting impossible standards
- Feeling threatened or insecure by people who are very successful
- Criticizing the failures of others in order to boost your own self-esteem

Any of this sound familiar?

If you're trapped in an all-or-nothing mindset, this is your sign to get out. To redefine your identity, person, and future.

When you look at the things that you've identified as most important—the ones you can't live without, the people and places and goals that are *everything* in your life—ask yourself this: **Why are they there?**

What would happen if you didn't hit your goals?

If you didn't get the job that you wanted, your business never took off, your partner changed their mind, or kids just never happened for you?

Because don't get me wrong, one of the big goals for this book is to give you, the reader, the tools and pieces that you need to create a life you love—but *it might not look the way that you want it to.*

I'm going to continue to encourage you to go for your goals, and hopefully equip you to do just that. But none of it matters unless you understand that your life is every bit as valuable whether or not you achieve everything you're dreaming of.

Building a life you love is almost a trick statement, because while you absolutely have the potential and the freedom to chase your dreams—and intentional living can help you do that effectively—it's not the attainment of those things that makes you love your life.

It's you.

Committing to it. Deciding to live differently. To find purpose in this place, right where you are, whatever it may look like.

All-or-nothing doesn't get you closer to the top. It keeps you on the bottom and removes the stairs. Yes, there are a few exceptions to this—but as a general rule, this mindset leads straight to bad burnout or keeps you from starting in the first place.

Unsurprisingly, this thought pattern is more present in people with anxiety disorders[1]. It kind of begs the whole chicken-and-egg question, given that it's an unbelievably stressful way to live.

You need to learn to separate who you are from what you've done, and particularly in the way that it's perceived by other people. Intentional living doesn't work when your intent is to look good, impress others, and show off—it's impossible to maintain and entirely out of your control.

Even when you are living the life you love—when you are your happiest and best self —even if you hit every goal on that list—there are going to be people who aren't your people. Who don't get it. Who have something to say, critique, or comment on.

The only way this works is if you know that you are whole on your own.

When you know who you are and what you're worth,

the fear of failure isn't so scary. The potential loss of one goal or accomplishment isn't such a big deal. It becomes easier to take a change in direction for what it is, rather than seeing it as a defeat.

Risk isn't your enemy.

One of the most fascinating parts of the Icarus story is often overshadowed by the boy's early death. Icarus' father, Daedalus, had an ending quite opposite from his son. As the story goes, Daedalus was able to keep a steady flight path.

Aside from the emotionally devastating loss of his son, Daedalus was fine. His wings carried him safely to Sicily, where his journey continued. He went on to continue his work as an inventor, and actually had a prolific career working for the king and creating public monuments.

Daedalus' risk was equal to his son's, and yet his journey went a completely different way.

Putting on the wings wasn't the problem.

It wasn't Icarus' flight that cost him his life, and I'd argue that it wasn't his ambition either.

The problem was a *lack of intentionality* behind his actions—he was missing the ability to weigh the risk against probable and potential outcomes, plan ahead, and invest time, energy, and resources in line with his purpose.

Certainty is less common than most of us would like, and some amount of risk is just inevitable. But rather than trying to avoid it, when you take chances on purpose, you give yourself the opportunity to put a plan, structure, or strategy in place.

Holding yourself back because you don't want to crash is like driving a car without holding the steering wheel. And I hate to break it to you, but there is no option to take your foot off the gas here—things are going to keep going, whether you like it or not. But when you take the wheel, your chance of crashing drops significantly.

You can choose which risks and routes to take, make wise decisions, consciously pursue uncertainty, and head into the future confident and prepared for whatever lies ahead.

Living on purpose requires you to take action. To know what you want and go for it, pursue the things that move your heart, and choose to make the most of every second.

Taking action & finding balance

Unlike an all-or-nothing mindset, intentional action doesn't require you to choose between procrastination or full speed ahead. But life on purpose can't be lived entirely in stillness.

Rest is not a bad thing—it's actually really important. Paralysis, on the other hand, gets you nowhere. When you spend too much time overthinking, obsessing, and getting caught up in the "what-ifs," you wind up holding yourself back from immeasurable potential. You don't know what you're capable of unless you try.

I almost didn't write this book because when I was 10, I wrote a different one.

I'd been an avid storyteller my whole life, with big dreams of becoming a successful author. My young self had finally completed what I was sure would be a big hit—a 40-page novel that I was immensely proud of.

For some reason, I expected that the release of this book would gain me a new kind of respect in society. I was proving what I could do, demonstrating my skill, and I saw wild fame and fortune in my future.

Needless to say—it didn't go that way.

Friends and family bought copies and told me how cute it was. The disparity between my expectations and reality left me devastated and determined to give up writing forever. The thought of publishing again was too humiliating to bear.

It sounds extremely melodramatic, but the reality is that at 10, I had placed my entire worth into that book without even meaning to. I defined myself by my writing, and when it didn't end up the way I expected it to, I literally didn't know who I was or how to move forward.

So I stopped writing. I adopted an all-or-nothing mindset, and between the all and the nothing, I chose nothing.

What had once been my passion, dream job, and main creative outlet was eliminated from my life, and I didn't write for pleasure again until I was 17.

Oddly enough, when I was in makeup school, I was presented with a couple of different opportunities to start writing again. I will always remember sitting in class when out of the blue, one of my classmates said, "Anika, you should start a blog."

Immediately, I had a sinking feeling, but not the bad kind. It was a—"What if that's what I'm supposed to be doing with my life?" moment, and it scared the crap out of me. I brushed it off and pushed it down, but I couldn't shake the thought.

The idea of writing *publicly* was paralyzing. Opening myself up to criticism, condescension, and the opinion of the world was a risk I did not want to take.

Over the next year, I had four people independently bring up the idea of starting a blog to me with no clue it had been on my mind. It was impossible to ignore, but nevertheless, the fear of failure was too much to take the risk.

As you know, the reason I'm writing this now is because I finally *did* start a blog. In late 2018, I launched my very first online writing project, which became *anikagreen.com,* which would go on to become *outofthehabit.com*.

That blog led to my first paid writing job, which led to my second and third, and as I sit here writing this, I can't believe I almost missed out on it.

I have *loved* writing my entire life. It's the thing I do that makes me feel the most *me.* It's how I interact best with my own thoughts, process my feelings and fears, and speak to the world. I am unbelievably grateful to wake up every day and get paid to learn, grow, and do what I feel like I was born to.

And I almost gave it up because I was *scared.*

Not everything I've tried has gone this well. Success was never (and still isn't) a guarantee. But the joy, the *passion*, and the life that has come from this for me would not have been possible if I hadn't worked up the nerve to take the first step.

To be clear, I didn't go all in right away. I'm not suggesting that the alternative to a "nothing" mindset is an "all." 100% and 0% are both bad ideas.

Finding a healthy balance between the two extremes allows you to *live.* It creates space for you to try, experiment, explore and see what comes of life. Whether it's a job you're scared to apply for, a program you're afraid to commit to, or a relationship with too much potential, when your knee-jerk reaction is to run from the things that scare you—*don't*.

Take a beat. Take a breath. And ask yourself if you're running because it's not what you want, or because the risk of failure—of rejection—is something you don't want to accept.

Having a vision is an invaluable step one. But the life you're dreaming of will never be within your reach unless you are willing to risk failing. You can't get from Point A to Point B by simply thinking about it.

Studies have shown that ultimately, at the end of their lives, people have much more regret over the things that they *didn't* do than over the things that they did[2].

Take the chance. Do the thing. Own your life and live without regrets over what you never tried to do.

Taking action is a fundamental requirement of an intentional life. By its very nature, it demands effort and choices and things that might scare you a little.

If this is new to you, or even if it's not, it's worth understanding the psychology behind this and some common misconceptions about what it looks like to take ownership of your life.

The Law of Attraction

The Law of Attraction is a common phenomenon and belief system in the personal development industry, defined by Psychology Today as "the belief that the universe creates and provides for you that which your thoughts are focused on."[3]

It's an extremely popular way of thinking that teaches that whatever you believe and dwell on will come to be in existence. It often involves things like daily affirmations, practicing manifestation (the act of willing something into existence), and a strong commitment to positive thinking. Positivity, according to the Law of Attraction, will always yield positive results.

The problem, though, is that this idea doesn't hold up.

A positive mindset is a great thing to have—it'll help you be more optimistic, enjoy life more, and get excited about the little things. Affirmations can help you change the way that you see yourself and your limitations, which can be really powerful, and as we've established, understanding where you want to go is key to achieving it.

But *it's not enough*.

Dreaming of financial freedom doesn't add to your bank account. Picturing your dream job doesn't qualify you for an interview, and thinking about your ideal partner won't bring them to you any faster.

These are good things, but they are all just step one. Just the beginning. Setting and creating the intent. When you end it there, you're giving up before you've even started.

In fact, the greatest danger of the law of attraction is that getting caught up in it can lead you to assume that you have no role in creating this life of yours. That your responsibility is simply to smile and wait.

This is just not true. Waiting for life to find you is the opposite of intentional living. Rather than pushing you towards purpose, potential, and growth, this reinforces complacency, passivity, and procrastination.

Optimism and complacency are not the same thing. If you want more than mediocrity out of your life, you *have* to be an active partner in it.

That doesn't mean constant blood, sweat, and tears, or that you should find yourself grinding all day every day. There is actually a way to make this easier on yourself by working with your brain, instincts, and natural tendencies to give yourself the best shot at your best life.

The role of the brain

There is a key element to the Law of Attraction that's actually a really, really good strategy for goal setting. Often used as proof of its legitimacy, a lot of people who actively practice "manifestation" have seen their dreams come into reality. I would argue, however, that this has a lot less to do with the universe than it does basic psychology.

There is powerful truth behind the idea that **if you believe you are capable of something, you are far more likely to accomplish it**. On the flip side, if you count yourself out before even trying, you ensure your failure. Henry Ford put it this way— "Whether you think you can or you think you can't, you're right."

The way you see yourself really does matter.

None of us are without limitations, but we often place them on ourselves prematurely. We decide that certain goals are beyond our reach, whether consciously or not, and either choose not to attempt them or sabotage our own progress along the way.

If you're constantly telling yourself why something *won't* work, you're not going to put in the time and effort to prove otherwise. You reap what you sow, and if you're sowing self-doubt, you'll end up sure that you were right all along.

It's just a rule that you will find whatever you expect to see around you. When you go through a breakup, you'll see your ex's car all over town. If you believe that there's no good people in the world, you'll unconsciously look for evidence of it. Deciding that you won't be able to stick to a routine, you'll watch yourself give up, and think "I knew it."

Confirmation bias is the brain's habit of searching for evidence to support what it already believes. This is a basic function of the mind, and while I hate to break it to you, it means that there's literally no way for you to see the world objectively.

When you build a vision board, make a goal list, or tell yourself things like "I will accomplish anything I set my mind to" enough, you start to believe them.

Over time, these subtle shifts in your beliefs will translate to action. You're more likely to ask for that raise (and get it) if you walk in feeling like you deserve it. You'll put the time and work into starting that business if you actually envision it being profitable. The way that you carry yourself and talk about what you do and think is all shaped and changed by your thoughts.

On a psychological level, your thoughts do change your environment. They literally alter the way you perceive things. The way you present yourself impacts the way that other people perceive you, and so on. Your mindset is really, really important—but a big part of why is because of how it impacts your actions.

It's for this reason that setting goals isn't enough, and why it matters how you do it. It's for this reason that the Law of Attraction isn't enough. The people who practice it and get results don't end up with success because it was handed to them—they end up with it because they started by believing it was possible and committed to seeing it through.

There's a reason why this book began with a chapter on vision casting—creating an idea of what you want life to be, developing a picture of where you want to go. Your goals *matter*—but strategies, systems, and action are what actually get you there.

What it means to take action

Have you ever felt passion so deep that you couldn't articulate it? Soul-stirring, perspective-shifting, emotion?

A love like never before, heartbreak beyond words, witnessing an injustice that you knew you'd never forget—passion can arise from a number of different circumstances and emotions. It looks different in all of us, but it's one of the most human experiences we can have.

Passion moves us, drives us, and changes us. It prompts a response. The things that we are most passionate about become part of who we are. They shape us, mold us, and lead us to a different kind of life.

To build on that car analogy (forgive me, my boyfriend is a car guy), you want purpose at the wheel and passion in the tank. Being fuelled by passion pushes your limits, and purpose redirects your focus to what's in front of you rather than what you think you can do.

Passion without some kind of direction or plan can lead to miscommunications, overreactions, and thoroughly overwhelming emotions—but when you embrace your passion as part of you, it becomes a source of energy and motivation.

One of the greatest mistakes I've made in trying to live intentionally was excluding the passions I already had from this dream life of mine.

I got caught up in the idea of what I thought an intentional life should look like, rather than what intentional living looked like *for me*. It's both a beautiful opportunity and a total pain that there is so much diversity in the application of purposeful living. I wanted someone to just tell me what to do, but I quickly learned that it doesn't really work like that.

How you take action in your life is going to largely depend somewhat on you and what your goals and ideas are. If you're feeling totally overwhelmed, stick with me for a minute—it's about to get a lot simpler.

Tempting as it may be for us planners, figuring out your whole life right now isn't an option—at least not a wise one. As important as it is to know your values, priorities, and goals, they'll probably play out in a number of different ways, many of which are likely impossible to even imagine right now.

Taking action does not require you to have it all figured out first—in fact, the reverse is probably true.

Too much of life is utterly unpredictable and completely unknown, so don't box yourself in, even as you work towards a specific vision. You may find that your goals change as you do. Your idea of success right now might be different from how it looks in two, five, or ten years.

Furthermore, your idea of *failure* will probably look different. See, the thing about failure is that despite Icarus' bitter end, things don't usually result in a plummeting death. Disappointment, maybe. Heartache, sure. But as much as risk isn't your enemy, *failure* isn't either.

Every groundbreaking, world-changing, legacy-making success has come after what could be considered a string of failures. Most people who discover how to do something right, first learn how to do it *wrong.*

It's in moments of failure that we are given the best opportunities to learn, grow, and discover that things were not what we thought. We get to embrace the journey, and accept that either something is not meant for us, or at least not in the way we wanted.

It sucks—but sometimes failure isn't even failure at all. It's life doing its thing, intentional living paying off, and a course redirection that, while it may not seem appealing right now, will ultimately lead you to where you are meant to be.

**Action doesn't lead you to failure.
It leads you to life.**

When you're pursuing the things that you value above all else, things tend to have a knack of working themselves out at some point or another.

Don't hold back from the unknown simply because it is an unknown. Live boldly, loudly, and unashamed in the pursuit of a life worth living.

CHAPTER THREE

How to Be an Enthusiast

What is an Enthusiast?

> *"I began to realize how important it was to be an enthusiast in life.... if you are interested in something, no matter what it is, go at it at full speed ahead. Embrace it with both arms, hug it, love it and above all become passionate about it. Lukewarm is no good. Hot is no good either. White hot and passionate is the only thing to be."*
>
> **Roald Dahl**

15 hours.
From the moment my alarm went off at 6 am, I was counting down.

I knew that as soon as my feet hit the floor, it would be exactly 15 hours before I could get back in bed. I checked the time constantly throughout the day, watching the hours slip by and feeling a rising sense of excitement.

14 hours. 12. 10.

By the time I sat down to dinner in the evenings, just a couple of short hours from my reward, I was downright *ecstatic.*

At that point in my life, I considered going to sleep the highlight of my day - which sounds more depressing than it was. I almost wish I could tell you that the attitude was justified, but while I was in a bit of a rough spot, a simple mindset shift would've done me a lot of good.

Remember that whole "the search for happiness is garbage" thing from the introduction? I still stand by that—basing your life on the pursuit of one particular feeling, particularly without a long-term strategy, makes no sense at all.

But also, life is short—and choosing purpose over temporary feelings doesn't mean you have to be miserable.

The term "enthusiast" is usually heard when attached to something else. A jazz enthusiast, a rock climbing enthusiast, an enthusiast of trombones or kazoos or Shakespeare or anything else. (Does the word enthusiast sound weird to you yet?)

The Oxford English Dictionary literally defines the word as "a person who is very interested in a particular activity or subject"[1]—specific, huh?

In this context, however, the word "enthusiast"

means to be a person who is very interested in *life itself*. An enthusiast is someone who gets excited about things that could be perceived as mundane or unimportant.

They're the friend you call with good news because you *know* they'll want to celebrate. The person who dives headfirst into their passion project and turns it into a side hustle. That friend you've got who gets way too excited about their favourite TV show (it's me, I'm the friend).

If this doesn't sound like you, don't stress. Even though you may not feel it right now, we all have some enthusiast roots—because the best example of an enthusiast is a child.

Think back to your early years, or take a look at children in your own life. Pay attention to what *thrills* them. Spoiler alert: it doesn't take much.

Now, this doesn't mean they're easily *satisfied* - of course, there are tantrums and tears and "how-dare-you-give-me-the-snack-I-just-asked-for", but the things that *light them up* are usually not all that complicated. Christmas morning, birthday parties, the ice cream truck—kids have this beautiful tendency to make a big deal out of everything.

These are the moments that they live for. And they're astonishingly simple.

Before they touch social media and cell phones, they have baseball in the backyard with a plastic bat and whiffle ball. A good game of hide and go seek. Bike rides around the neighbourhood.

And it's enough for them.

Not all of us had idyllic childhoods, but everyone who was once young knows what it's like to experience the rush of a simple joy. Childhood comes with this innate enthusiasm and freedom to feel whatever hits you.

Somewhere between infancy and adulthood, this freedom is usually lost. Instead of being taught how to manage our feelings, we often learn to push them down. We shrink them, minimize them, and ignore them—and then we become adults who too often miss the beauty in the big-ness of everything.

We look at the tears and tantrums and say things like "calm down" or "it's not a big deal." We see the overjoyed, over-reactive celebrations and laugh. Because it's *cute*— rather than joining in.

We forget that we are being watched, every second, by little eyes and hearts and minds, who are picking up on messages that we don't even mean to send.

Learning to be an enthusiast means reigniting this part of yourself.

Getting in touch with childlike wonder, excitement, and passion—whatever it looks like in your life. You don't have to go nuts on Christmas morning or chase the ice cream truck down the street, but when you find yourself falling in love with something, do it with all of you.

Throw the party. Get excited. Dream about the future and the present and remember what it's like to feel hope in the little things. How pizza and a movie made you feel like you were on top of the world, or how learning a new skill would boost your confidence like nothing else.

While all-or-nothing thinking usually doesn't lead anywhere good, there's something to be said for putting your heart and soul into things that matter to you.

This is particularly important when it comes to things like work or relationships. Anything that takes up consistent time and emotions in everyday life is, by nature, a priority. And if you can't invest deeply in the most significant things in your life, it might be time to reevaluate them.

Not every job you take will be a dream one or a passion project, but it's in those situations that enthusiasm is so key.

That season of my life, counting down the hours until I could crash, was miserable.

Weeks turned to months and nothing was changing— except the weather, and if you know anything about Winter in Vancouver, you know it is liquid misery— non-stop bone-chilling rain for months at a time.

I was constantly sad and sick of it—so I started what I thought was a little game for myself, but what ended up becoming a life-changing habit that forever altered how I saw the world.

Every day, when I woke up, I had one goal before I got out of bed. My feet weren't allowed to hit the floor until I had thought of one thing to look forward to that day. Sometimes it was buying a coffee out, other times it was watching a Christmas movie by myself, but no matter what, I could think of one thing. The rule was that it had to be something in my control. I didn't want to base my good mood on someone else's actions or choices, that was too unpredictable.

Whatever I selected, it was my responsibility. This exercise gave me something to look forward to throughout the day and helped get my mind in a healthier spot. Over time, it became a habit that I performed without even thinking about it, and to this day, I usually find myself listing things to look forward to before I've even cracked my eyes open.

Enthusiasm is not about figuring it all out or immersing yourself in happy situations. It gives you no more control over life than you have right now. It's not a personality type. Enthusiasm will not help you ignore negative feelings or experiences, and it's definitely not a shortcut to instant gratification.

Rather, enthusiasts are individuals who have learned the art of creating their own joy in any circumstance.

It doesn't matter what path you take, things are going to go wrong sometimes. You could be the most intentional person in the world, and life will still hit you out of nowhere. There isn't a way to escape the unexpected, which is why it's so dangerous to place your ability to be happy in things you can't control.

Enthusiasm doesn't have to be compartmentalized—limited to one passion or hobby. It can be cultivated, practiced, and made habitual. Turned into instinct. Instead of waking up to count down the hours of your day, can you imagine how much fun life would be if you spent your time actually *excited* about everything that you were doing?

Enthusiasm is more than optimism. It's not blind positivity or ignorance of reality.

Where an enthusiast finds no reason for joy, they create one.

I recognize that this can be an oversimplification and that in saying this, my own privilege and 2021 western worldview are showing. I get that. And I'm not suggesting that a movie night or a pumpkin spiced latte will fix real trauma or hardship.

This mindset was not always a part of my life, and is

something I've had to learn to implement in the last several years.

Not everything in life is fixed with a smile and a spoonful of sugar. Even if you mastered enthusiasm overnight, injustice and loss and pain would still be present in the world and in your life. There is no mindset shift, inspirational quote, or growth journey that could change that.

In fact, it's because of this reality, and not in spite of it, that enthusiasm is a far superior and much more effective mindset than typical positivity.

Enthusiasm > positivity

To clarify, positivity is most definitely not a bad thing. An optimistic outlook on life comes with a long list of benefits, including a lower likelihood of depression, better coping skills, and a longer life span.[2] The problem lies in relying on positivity or optimism to get you through the day because they are far too easily disproved.

An overly positive mentality tells you to ignore the negative, slap on a Stepford-like smile, and always assume and expect the best.

But when life gets real, things go wrong, and the unthinkable happens, you are left empty-handed.

A smile on your face doesn't make right the wrong that's been done to you, and a bubble bath and face mask won't cure your heartache. Positivity is a beneficial trait, not a treatment for serious hurt.

Enthusiasm brings a much-needed balance to the conversation of positivity versus negativity. The idea behind it is simple—finding and creating the best in life without ignoring the worst.

Running from painful realities does you no good. It leaves no room for emotional balance, development, or healing.

Positivity is *built* on a need for happiness, and it relies heavily on satisfaction as your primary goal. With this outlook, there is a deeply personal responsibility to be happy all of the time—and if you're not, it's definitely your fault.

This way of thinking tells you to cut out anything that doesn't make you happy. It insists on a me-first mindset at all times, and it *thrives* when coupled with—you guessed it—the search for happiness instant gratification.

And the thing is, that doesn't sound so bad at first. It's actually all well and fine for a bit, and then you turn on the news,

Or you lose a job,

Or you lose a friend,

or a relationship ends out of the blue, and all of a sudden, *that doesn't work anymore.*

When life gets hard, positivity is not the foundation you want to be standing on. Positivity is not the friend telling you "This is really hard, but you are going to get through this," it's the unwelcome stranger telling you that "Everything happens for a reason."

Not only is this hurtful, it's a terribly unhealthy way to live. It is really, really important to understand the difference here between positivity and enthusiasm.

An enthusiast mindset, at least one built into intentional living, doesn't rely on forced feelings or false happiness.

It doesn't suggest that you're always going to be cheerful, and instead creates space for you to feel whatever you're feeling while giving you the tools not to stay stuck in it.

Enthusiasm doesn't dwell on the negative, but finds peace in it. Rather than avoiding the inevitable or hopelessly relying on quick hits of endorphins, this way of living allows you to develop healthy coping mechanisms and actually heal from what you experience.

Just like intentional living as a whole, enthusiasm will play out differently based on your preferences, personality type, life stage, and loves. Your greatest joys and excitements in life will be different from the people around you. Your heart, mind, and person are totally unique.

This is a bold shift, and one with the potential to change the way that you interact with everything around you. It's uncommon, completely contagious, and a total blast.

Why *not* live this way—full speed ahead, arms wide open, ready to embrace the things ahead of you? On *fire* and elated by the everyday.

Becoming an enthusiast is one of the greatest things I have ever done, and there are few acts of growth that can top the impact it has had in my life. Rather than counting down the hours until I can get back in bed, I actually wake up looking forward to the day. It took some time, but I am able to find joy in the most menial of tasks, even if I don't always look forward to them.

Enthusiastic living is accomplished through a series of little steps, practices, and habits—and while you'll probably develop some for yourself, I've found these to be the absolute best place to start.

How to Become an Enthusiast
Celebrate the little things

Step one to becoming an enthusiast: celebrate *everything.*

One of the greatest tragedies in life is to never realize the fullness of what's around you. We don't even see, much less celebrate the people, places, and life events around us. Even our own accomplishments often go unnoticed. In stark contrast to childhood wonder, adulthood often comes with the habit of shoving things down. We push away any big feelings, even happy ones, making them smaller and smaller until they fit into a box we are comfortable with.

Enthusiasm does the opposite.

Rather than being reserved for special occasions or events, celebration becomes a way of life and a form of connection, both with others and to yourself. It comes with permission to live fully *now*, rather than waiting to hit a particular standard or level.

Finished a big project at work? WAY TO GO. Treat yourself to a night out.

Hit a weekly workout goal? Feel good about that!

Stepped out of your comfort zone? AMAZING. So proud of you.

You're too old for a birthday party? Throw one anyway.

An enthusiastic life isn't necessarily big or flashy. It's just full. It grabs hold of the good and stretches it rather than shrinking. Enthusiasm actively, actionably seeks out the best parts of life and multiplies them.

One of the biggest obstacles to embracing this mindset is that it almost requires a certain level of healthy self-esteem. Celebrating yourself feels really, really awkward when you don't feel great about who you are. Confidence isn't exactly built into most of us today, which is all the more reason why getting comfortable with this is so very important.

Celebrating yourself doesn't need to be cocky or pushy. Arrogant celebration is "I have to be the best." It's holding yourself up to other people, comparing your value, accomplishments, and place in life to someone else. Celebrating yourself *so that* other people notice. It's competitive and unkind.

Confident, healthy celebration is "I'm proud of what I did." Celebrating the wins that are wins for you without making your progress a mile marker for others. Recognizing your own growth, development, and achievements. It's reflective, intentional, and powerful.

This kind of celebration flows out of a place of joy (or enthusiasm), whereas arrogant celebration comes from insecurity—a need to prove yourself and show what you're worth.

This is a *massive* distinction.

When you know your worth, you don't need to prove it to other people.

Practicing healthy celebration and developing healthy self-esteem go hand in hand, each contributing to and benefitting the other.

This isn't dismissal or denial of the very real pain and hardships of life. For every loss, grief, and disappointment, there are wins, successes, and reasons to celebrate. But without a conscious intent to see them, they often slip by, leaving us to focus on the dark.

The world is messy and complicated and unjust, and in adopting an intentional mindset, I hope you are moved to fight against the things that are heavy in your heart. But honestly, you will be more effective, productive, and successful if you can also learn to see the wins.

Celebrating the little things often gets a bad rap because people assume it requires turning a blind eye to the hard ones. This is just not true.

Habitually finding reasons to celebrate is one of the best ways to better yourself and your quality of life, both of which affect your ability to contribute to the world around you.

Easy ways to celebrate the little things

- When you set a goal, pick something to do as a reward after hitting it, and when you do, make sure to follow through.
- Call a friend and tell them about something good that just happened.
- Make a social media post about what helped you accomplish something recently.
- Surprise someone you love with flowers or a coffee just because of who they are.
- Plan things to look forward to ahead of time.

- Don't stress too hard about the small stuff.
- Let go of your mistakes. You can't take them back.
- Find times to treat yourself for no particular reason.

Recently, I was talking to someone who told me about how they're learning the value of even just acknowledging when they finish something. A task, a project, a challenge.

It's so easy to get caught up in the hustle of everyday life and lose track of what we're doing. We finish one task, and immediately start stressing or focusing on the next one. But what if we didn't?

What if we stopped?

What if we took a second to just acknowledge the work we put in, pat ourselves on the back, and be *proud* of what we did? It's a small thing, but it can change how you see yourself and your worth.

If celebrating yourself feels totally out of your comfort zone, maybe this is a good place to start. Simply taking the time to see and acknowledge what you've done and the work you've put into something before moving on to what's next.

On an everyday basis, the art of celebration can transform your attitude, heart, and expectations towards your day. When you wake up in the morning, decide to be in a good mood. If you need a reason, think of one. What's one thing that you can do, create, or look forward to?

If you don't have something already planned, plan it before you even get it out of bed. Pick up your favourite hot drink on the way to work, ask a friend to meet you for dinner, schedule an at-home movie night or take a long bath with a good book.

Whatever it is for you, hold onto it. Carry it with you throughout your day, remember the joy in the simplicity of it, and repeat it the next morning. It sounds a little trivial, but the more you do an action, the more instinctual it becomes (more on this later).

Find a purpose outside of yourself

One of the best strategies for enthusiasm—and for intentional living altogether—is to find a purpose outside of yourself.

Purpose is central to who you are and what you do.

But did you know that purpose that's not about *you* is actually more effective?

Whether you woke up on the wrong side of the bed, you're unhappy with your current circumstance, or it's just one of those days where everything is going wrong, one of the fastest and best ways to turn things around is to find an altruistic purpose. An intent that has nothing to do with your own benefit.

Not only do altruistic people live longer, healthier, happier lives,[3] but simple acts of sacrifice usually act as an instant mood boost. Helping other people makes us *feel good*, and it takes the focus off of ourselves.

Humans are selfish creatures. We don't like to admit it, but there's no escaping it, and it's impossible to change your innate wiring. When faced with the choice to do something you enjoy vs. something you don't, you will always want to do the thing that sounds good. We are wired to seek pleasure and avoid pain. Rather than working against yourself, start training your brain to take pleasure in things that you want to do anyway.

Make your own bright side

Six weeks after graduating from high school, I moved 9 hours away from everyone that I knew to pursue a career in makeup artistry. It had been a passion of mine for years, and it was finally happening.

In the year leading up to it, I'd endured snarky comments, criticisms, and interventions from concerned individuals who told me I was ruining my life. I'll never forget the high of finding out that I'd won a competitive scholarship, only to be pulled aside by a high school teacher who told me I wouldn't be able to use it because there was *no* way my school was accredited (it was).

As insane as it drove me, there was nothing that

could have motivated me more. I have always been stubborn, particularly when someone tells me I'm not capable of something. Every bone in my body becomes focused on proving them wrong.

I worked hard all year, honing my skills, preparing for the move, and dreaming of what my life would be like when I'd made it.

And off I went, confident beyond reason that this was my calling in life.

If the fact that I now write for a living hadn't already tipped you off, let me tell you—I was wrong.

The first few months of the program were great, and I was still committed to my plan and my path, but eventually, I began to realize that while I did love makeup artistry, it wasn't what I wanted to do as a career.

My original goal had been to go into the film industry. I have undying respect for the incredible artists who do just that, but the lifestyle wasn't something I was willing to commit to. In order to fulfill that dream, I would have to prioritize it over things like travelling, getting involved in my community, etc.

It's not that those things were impossible, but they couldn't all be a priority.

This was the first time it had ever occurred to me to build some kind of intentionality into my life and goals. Until that point, most things had been decided for me.

While my experience in makeup school didn't end in a career, it taught me more than I could've imagined about the power of the bright side.

It was about halfway through the year that I realized this wasn't for me. At that point, I was really struggling. Being so far from my family, with few friends and no real sense of community was incredibly lonely, and time and time again, I almost gave up.

I got to a point where I was desperate. Miserable, unhappy, and bitter. I knew I had a terrible attitude, and there was no way that I could make it to the end of the year feeling like that. So, the way I saw it, I had two options:

1. I could give up. Drop out, go home, nurse a wounded ego and try to pick up the pieces of a shattered vision for the future. This option was unappealing, largely because going home meant facing everyone who'd predicted my failure—and that thought made me sick to my stomach.

2. I could suck it up. Place my trust and faith in God's plan, ask Him to get me through the year, and start finding reasons to be happy. I had little control over my circumstances and schedule, but my mindset was my own, and I could work really, really hard to change that.

It's because I chose option 2 that I'm writing this

book. That I began to gain an understanding of what it means to live on purpose. And it was through this act that I began developing the habit of creating my own bright side for things.

If I wasn't at school, I had to work, which made it really hard to meet friends. So I started getting to know my coworkers more, and soon developed meaningful friendships that have lasted years.

The church across the street from my house wasn't the right fit for me, so I started getting up earlier and bussing an hour each way to a church that would eventually transform my faith, provide work opportunities, and introduce me to my now best friends and boyfriend.

The hard things were still hard. Creating a bright side didn't make my family closer, pay off my student loans, or restore my pride. But rather than sitting in misery, I could focus on getting excited about the positive changes in my life.

In all likelihood, you have more power than you think you do.

Your situation may be unchanging, but I'm almost positive that there are probably chances for you to explore something fun, exciting, or positive—even if it's entirely unrelated to the difficult things.

As hard as it can be to hear, a victim mindset is natural for a lot of us. We reach for the woe-is-me card before even thinking about what we can do to change things on our own.

But while sulking might feel satisfying in the moment, it does you no good in the long run.

The only person who can keep you from becoming who you want to be is you.

The world can feel heavy and loud sometimes, but you don't have to stay in the noise. Slow down and take the time to celebrate life. The breath in your lungs, the weather, the people around you, and the roof over your head. Get excited about the good things. Find ways to encourage other people. **And when things start feeling dark, either find the light, or be it.**

Try new things

In order to become an enthusiast, you need to get used to trying new things. Breaking out of a mold, saying "yes" to the unknown, and embracing unavoidable uncertainty. New experiences aren't just about the moments themselves, but about learning what it's like to really *live.*

A few years ago, there was this quote from Neale Donald Walsch that was plastered on every t-shirt, computer wallpaper, and Tumblr page—"Life begins at the end of your comfort zone."

I have a vivid memory of my teenage self rolling

my eyes at the words, writing it off as a cheesy line. And it is, but there's also some really powerful truth behind it.

Your comfort zone is made up of the things that you know. It's safe, certain, and, well, comfortable. When you are in it, things are simpler. It's easier to be yourself, you can relax, and while stress may be present, it's not overwhelming.

It's *easy*.

Now, to be clear, your comfort zone is a necessary part of who you are. It's not your enemy, and doing things that feel safe is by all means encouraged.

The aim in trying new things is not to destroy your comfort zone, but to expand it.

From the moment you are born, the limits of your comfort zone are flexible. As an infant, toddler, and child, you are constantly exposed to things that are out of your comfort zone. (Kinda gives you a bit of sympathy for overwhelmed toddlers to think about it this way, doesn't it?) New people, places, and experiences are thrown at you every day, but over time, they start to become normal.

The early years of your life are exploding with the unknown. But over time, you get used to the basics.

Your comfort zone stops expanding. The limits are perceived as less flexible, and the unknown, more dangerous. Over time, many people simply stop trying new things altogether.

But what kind of life is that?

When you stop trying new things, you limit yourself, your mind, and your future. You hold back passion, joy, and love that is only unlocked through experiencing things for the first time. You miss out on so many opportunities to live, simply because you don't know what you're missing.

As we've already established, life has a certain kind of unpredictableness, meaning that it's impossible to avoid new things altogether. Even if it scares you entirely, you will at times be forced into newness. So really, all you're doing is holding yourself back from the fun of it.

Trying new things helps to keep you motivated, allowing you to reach what psychologists call "optimal anxiety."[4] Optimal Anxiety is what happens when you take a risk or try something new. It's just enough of a push that your brain and body jump into gear—you perform well in whatever you're doing without so much stress that you shut down.

Routines are important, but so is breaking the— experimenting with new hobbies, habits, and parts of life.

The simple act of learning - in any context - *requires* you to experience the unknown. By definition, you know something that you didn't before. In fact, a Yale study[5] actually proved that stability works against your ability to learn—so much so that it literally triggers a kind of shut-off switch.

When faced with what you don't know, your brain lights up, ready to engage and explore the possibilities. But over time, watching the same outcome over and over starts to dull your mind. You're less engaged. Less curious. And less invested in what's going on around you.

Your future depends largely on how you approach the unknown. These big dreams and goals of yours are going to require moments of boldness, steps of bravery, and confidence in exploration.

Falling in love, finding your passions, and building the life of your dreams all require you to step out of your "normal" a little. To dare to do something uncomfortable. Starting the habit now prepares you to do this in the best way possible.

Get passionate

I'm a firm believer that there is always something to get excited about. It just takes some practice learning to look for it. It's not necessarily about shifting your lifestyle or investing large amounts of time/finances to find something more satisfying. You can get excited about having good coffee in the morning. Wearing your favourite shirt. Driving in the rain because it reminds you of New York City in the fall.

Your circumstances, job, relationship status, or emotions may not be within your control, at least in the sense of instant change—but your attitude is. You are responsible for the ways in which you interact with the world around you and what imprints you leave on it.

A key part of living life as an enthusiast is giving yourself space to fully explore and embrace the things you love. To feel things deeply, even if it seems silly or small.

For example: I love *The Office.* I quote it at least three times a day. I've watched it more times than I can count, and when I thought "What am I passionate about?" it's one of the first three things that popped into my head. And I am passionate about it. I think the writing is fantastic. I love the character development. and I'm constantly impressed by how detailed it is. Additionally, it's not your basic sitcom, ripping off the same scenarios over and over again.

Yeah, it's a TV show. (To clarify—TV consumption is never a top priority in my life, and is used as a winding-down, fun activity, not a preferred lifestyle.) But I love *The Office*, and it's something that I can get excited about.

How often do you go all in? Whether it's directed towards a relationship, a TV show, book, or career, give yourself permission to fully enjoy the things that you love. Two feet in.

Lukewarm is no good.

Hopefully this goes without saying, but use discretion here. The things you're passionate about can become a part of you, but loving fully is something people rarely regret.

Give yourself grace

Enthusiasm isn't a switch you flip on and off. It's a mindset like anything else, and these practices are most effective when they become habits.

You'll still experience disappointment, feel negative feelings, and have days when you wake up in a bad mood. But herein lies the beautiful, beautiful nature of habitual behaviour change.

When you repeat an action often enough, even if it's just a thought pattern, you develop a kind of muscle memory.

Things like seeing the good, celebrating the little things, and creating your own joy become instinctual. It's not something you're doing, it's something you **are.**

Enthusiasm takes practice. If it's not your natural bent, it can seem childish or weird to think about getting hyped over a great cup of coffee or asking a coworker how their day was. These seemingly small actions don't always become instant cause for celebration, and that's okay.

But over time, it will become easier, and eventually, it will become **you.**

The point isn't really about the details of your situation. It's developing the practice of taking ownership of your own joy and getting passionate. Recognizing the hardships in life and choosing not to let them run things.

Rather than toxic positivity, which tells you to ignore the bad, or put a positive spin on things that are just tragic, enthusiasm encourages balanced, realistic, intentional joy. It makes the great greater and helps take away from the sting of the bad.

For those of us who naturally tend to see the worst in everything (hey-o), this is completely foreign. It might not even seem appealing yet. But I can promise you that not only does it make life more fun, it's one of the most empowering things that you can possibly do for yourself.

Intentional living gives you the tools to create and own the narrative of your life.

You get to redefine what things look like for you, and especially after hardship, this is huge.

Lifelong patterns don't change overnight, so don't expect to go from 0 to 100. We're shooting for sustainability here, so cast a wide net and see what you come up with. Try lots of different things. Maybe work on implementing a different action step every week and see what you want to stick with.

Whatever you do, have fun with it. Give yourself

grace to grow at your own rate and discover the things that work for you. Any real change in your life will take time to sink in, so don't beat yourself up for falling into old habits, just change the thought and move on.

Romanticize your life a bit, but *stay grounded.* Don't place all of your joy and excitement on big, unpredictable things that aren't in your control. Remember what matters most in your life, and keep your priorities straight.

Notice the things that make you feel alive, and find new ways to increase their presence in your life.

Press into the things that light you up.

To live like an enthusiast takes intentionality, practice, and determination. There's no magic button that makes you happier overnight. If you're feeling stuck in a rut, bored, or unhappy with your day-to-day, give an enthusiastic mindset a shot.

Above all, remember that becoming better is rarely accidental—so stay consistent in your pursuit of a life you love. Enthusiasm is a daily choice, as is inten-tionality—it's up to you to make it.

CHAPTER FOUR:
Goals

I love New Year's Resolutions.

It's such a beautiful idea. Sitting down at the end of a year, reflecting on what it's been and dreaming about what could be next. It's a chance to cultivate gratitude, to remember what you learned, and to pursue growth. When it's done well, it can be a life-changing ritual.

Goal setting is a really powerful thing, but it often gets a bad rap as an ineffective way to change your life. And the fact is, approximately 80%[1] of people fail to keep their New Year's Resolutions.

Those dreams of what's ahead, the growth goals they passionately believed in on January 1st are often abandoned within the first month.

And for this, some criticism is fair. Most goals that are set during this time aren't successful, but the problem is the method, not goal-setting itself. If you want to grow or improve your life over any period of time, a target is necessary. It gives you direction, guidance, and clarity on what to prioritize.

A vision board, resolution, or goal tracker isn't enough to transform your life in and of itself. Without follow-through, those things are just wishful thinking. You can't hack your way to an authentic, intentional life.

But goals *are* important, especially in a purposeful life. They hold you accountable, help you stay motivated, and keep you on track for the life you want to create.

The difference between being a part of the 80% who fail and the 20% who don't is knowing how to set successful goals.

What is a successful goal?

I am personally of the opinion that the average goal fails because of two reasons. One, it's set with no attainable plan of action (and therefore met with no follow-through) or two, the goal was an unsuccessful one from the start.

While you are likely capable of more than you know, not all goals are ones you can hit—at least not in the way you might go about setting them. Setting successful goals means understanding what you can do, how hard to push yourself, and how to set yourself up for a win.

Contrary to popular belief, goals don't usually fail (or

succeed) because of willpower. A major life change requires more than just wanting it bad enough. There are a number of factors that impact the outcome of your goal, and not all of them are up to you. Support, logistics, timing and relationships all have a part to play.

Not everything is about motivation. This is a hard lesson to learn, especially if you tend to beat yourself up for missing a target. Successful goals are a lot more strategic than you might think. Setting goals that work is not about forcing yourself to do something over and over, but rather building a system that makes it easy for you to shift.

One of the weirdest ways to embark on a journey of self-improvement is to make it really, really hard for yourself.

And yet, it's a pretty typical way to approach it.

The reality is that the goals you set—at least the short-term ones—shouldn't be *that* hard. Now, don't get me wrong, big vision for the future is a good thing. Set your sights as high as you want. But be honest about where you're at right now and what it would look like to get there.

Setting unrealistic expectations only leads to disappointment, which isn't particularly motivating.

At the start of 2021, I set an absolutely ridiculous New Year's Resolution. My goal was to read one book every week for the year. I posted about it on

Instagram, made a reading list, and decided to commit.

Now, the idea of reading 52 books in a year doesn't sound that wild—until you understand that I read two books in 2020. Two.

I'm generally a fast reader, but it had been years since I'd read for pleasure, and I had absolutely no business thinking it would be an easy thing to crush. I read at least a little every day for the first week - and then life got busy and crazy and this new, unrealistic goal that I knew I'd never hit was the first thing to get dropped.

Halfway through the year, I'd read exactly *one* book. And to be honest, I only finished that one because I had to quarantine and was bored out of my mind.

After an interruption in my progress, I didn't have any motivation or desire to keep going. It was an all-or-nothing mindset moment. Why push into a goal that was so big and overwhelming only to fail?

The happy ending to that story is that later in the year, I did actually pick up reading again. Over the summer, I got hooked on a fiction book for the first time in years, and it set off a chain reaction. I generally average a book a week right now, but I'm not tracking it, and honestly, I don't really care.

The point of the goal wasn't the number, it was to get back in touch with a healthy habit and hobby that I really do love. If I had simply made *that* the goal in and of itself, I probably would have hit the number anyways.

When you meet serious resistance in working towards a goal, it's hard to keep going. The harder it is, the less your goal seems worth it. Before long, you may find yourself abandoning the thing entirely.

On the other hand, successful goals are typically smaller, realistic, and provide just enough of a challenge to give you a win without creating so much difficulty that you're tempted to abandon them. The exact goals that you set will be unique to you, but to give you a baseline, here are some characteristics of typical, successful goals:

1. Successful goals should be **available**.

Before you decide to challenge yourself in a specific way, take a second to think about what this is actually going to look like. If you want to spend less time on social media, but you're about to launch a product for your online business, deleting Instagram from your phone for a week might not be a goal that's available to you—it's just not a good option.

This doesn't mean you abandon the desired result, it just means finding a more practical way to implement it. For example, you could try turning off your phone at 8 pm every night, or look into hiring a social media manager to handle the account. Your goal needs to actually be a sustainable option for you. Think about your life in general, but also the specific season you're in—it's okay to wait a little bit to jump into something if it's just not doable right now.

2. Successful goals should be **realistic**.

In the same way that going "cold turkey" from something feels abrasive, unhelpful, and impossible to stick to, going "all-in" overnight on something doesn't set you up for a consistent lifestyle. If you haven't read a book for fun in years, giving yourself the goal of knocking out one a week might be *technically* doable, but it isn't realistic (talking to myself here).

I often find these kinds of targets tempting, because they sound really impressive. I think of how cool it would be to actually hit them. How good the bragging rights would sound, how impressed other people would be.

But it's not conducive to successful goal setting. Give yourself grace and stay focused on why you're setting this goal in the first place.

3. Successful goals should be **fun.**

You should enjoy the challenge and the experience of the wins, even if the actions themselves aren't your first choice. When you complete a goal you set, big or small, it's cause for celebration! Be proud of yourself for every step that you take. You are building into the life you want to live and the person that you want to become. You are much more likely to stick to your goals when you can celebrate them and see them as wins, too.

4. Successful goals should be **systematic**.

Part of the reason that goal setting can have such a negative reputation is because when it's done poorly, it doesn't get you anywhere. Giving yourself a one time target—running a 5k, eating one healthy meal this week - is useless unless you see it as part of something bigger. Crossing off that one goal might feel good, but when it's over, your life is the same, and there's no lasting change.

When you set a goal, make sure that you know, even just for yourself, what its role is in the larger vision that you have for your life.

Is this going to become a regular habit?

Are you building up to a more intense version of this?

The goals you set matter. The way you see yourself and your progress matters.

Doing this well means *acknowledging your own imperfections as well as the chaos of life, and finding a system that supports you enough to withstand it.*

The more you practice goal setting, the more you'll start to figure out what works and what doesn't. Pay attention to your preferences and what motivates, inspires, and encourages you.

As you set short-term targets and begin working towards them, keep in mind that while setting successful goals is a *huge* win, the execution is what gets you the rest of the way there.

How to Hit Successful Goals
Translating long-term goals into actionable ideas

When you look over your long-term goals—5 years, 20 years, the legacy you want to leave, they probably feel very far away. In a sense, they are, at least from being fully realized. The thing with long-term goals, though, is that they require long-term action. Hitting them means starting to work towards them well before their due date.

The best way to set yourself up to hit a long-term goal is to break it down, step by step, into realistic, actionable ideas. In his bestselling book *Atomic Habits,*2 James Clear talks about the practical goal of slowly and consistently improving yourself. Rather than trying to go from 0 to 100, focus on becoming better by 1% every day.

It doesn't sound like much, but the impact after a year of this is significant—and if, in contrast, you were to get 1% *worse* every day, the impact would be just as drastic.

If you want to make a big career change this year, making it your goal to "find a new job" might not be your best bet. At least, not if you end it there. The new job might be your ultimate goal, but without any smaller goals or action steps to getting there, it's going to be a lot harder—and probably messy.

Instead of leaving it there, you could break this down into easier, more attainable steps with a timeline you can commit to.

Maybe step one is doing research on other options. Watching YouTube videos, reading books, connecting with friends to get some information about what you may want to do. This stage is just about gathering information and spending time intentionally looking at opportunities.

Step two might be to look into the logistics of a job type that you're considering. Pay structure, average salary. Are there local openings for this position? Or would it require you to relocate?

Step three could be actually applying for these jobs, and finally, you would shoot to make the transition. You could give yourself ongoing things to keep in mind, too, like soaking up whatever development and skill training you can get at your current job before leaving.

One of my long-term goals is to be in a healthy, intentional, loving relationship. You know, that can't-eat, can't-sleep, reach-for-the-stars, over-the-fence, World series kind of stuff[3].

That goal isn't something I can just check off of a to-do list, and it's definitely not something that happens overnight. But it's a target that my boyfriend and I share. As a priority to both of us, we've implemented several regular practices in our everyday lives that help us work towards it.

1. **We say "I love you" every day.** It's never withheld, even in arguments or moments of conflict—love isn't manipulated or used as a bargaining chip.

2. **We communicate expectations and needs.** I'm definitely growing in this—I have come *so* far over the course of our relationship at being able to express what I need. I had a really hard time asking for help when we first started dating. Eventually, through focusing on taking little steps and getting just a bit better every day, this aspect of our relationship has become much stronger.

3. **We have fun together.** No matter how stressful things get, or how crazy our lives are, we never fail to make time for enjoying each other's company.

4. **We try to do a weekly date night** (sometimes that's an evening out, other times it's playing video games on the couch with a bottle of wine). Once a month, we have a planning night, where we go through our budgets, calendars, and any life events planned for the next few weeks. This helps communication and creates space for us to be on the same page about expectations.

Experiment with this method for some of your long-term goals, and see what you come up with. Don't try to do everything at once. Overwhelming yourself is one of the most effective ways to guarantee you won't stick with something, so go slow and pick one goal at a time.

Something I've found extremely helpful is the practice of monthly goal setting—reevaluating my habits, priorities, and targets on a consistent basis. I have overarching, long-term goals, but every month, I like to sit down and give myself smaller things to shoot for. On its own, this won't get you everywhere you want to go —but when executed properly, monthly goal setting can serve as a catalyst for success.

Know your why

Keeping *purpose* at the forefront of your mind and motivation is absolutely central to hitting your goals. Without knowing why you're doing the little things, they become easy to skip and write off. Why bother cooking a healthy meal, doing something nice for your partner, or going for a walk tonight? It's just once, it's no big deal to skip.

Doing it because you have to or because you feel like you *should* doesn't work. Once or twice, maybe you can guilt yourself into it. But on an ongoing basis, you need something real, deep, and strong. A powerful sense of who and what you're doing this for. Know your why, and keep it close to you. Write it down, refer back to it, and remind yourself that this is an opportunity, not a punishment.

Each and every small-term goal that you set has a role in your larger vision for your life—so what's yours?

The goals that you set need to matter to you. Relying on feeling motivated to get you somewhere isn't a good strategy, but at the same time, you need some kind of emotional buy-in in order to stick it out. Working towards goals is a great feeling, but inevitably, you'll have some hard days.

When those come, you need to know why you're doing what you're doing and the ways that it will all be worth it in the end.

Track it

Goal tracking is one of the easiest ways to make your goal-setting a more successful process. The simple act of writing down your goals massively impacts your chances of hitting them. A Harvard study[4] actually discovered that just ten years after graduating, the 3% of their MBA grads who wrote down their goals were more successful than the other 97% *combined.*

When you get an idea out of your head, especially when you're putting it onto paper, it takes on a new kind of life and commitment. Somehow, the unlikely becomes more possible, and rather than toying with an idea, you're choosing to pursue it.

Particularly if you're a visual or kinesthetic person, goal tracking is a great way to stay dedicated to your task and also see the progress that you're making. On the days you don't feel motivated, it goes a long way to see actual evidence of your work. You can find a more detailed explanation of how to do this at *outofthehabit.com*, and either use a notebook, journal, or the free downloadable Goal Tracker available at *outofthehabit.com/printables*.

Precommit yourself to good decisions

A couple of months ago, I heard a TEDTalk from behavioural scientist Wendy De La Rosa on psychological tricks to help you save money[5]. It's genius, and I do mean *genius*. The principles she teaches apply to any area of life, particularly when it comes to growth and goal setting.

One of the ideas that has stuck with me the most is what De La Rosa calls "harnessing the power of precommitment." See, we tend to idealize our future selves a bit—the ones who've done all the work. We think of our future selves as people who always make the right decisions, who've built the right habits, and know how to do what needs to get done.

But our future selves are the same people that we are.

The only way to become a better version of yourself

is to start becoming them now. You don't go from beginner to pro overnight, and new habits in your life will take time to adopt.

Precommitment is a great way to do just that.

Whenever possible, look for opportunities to set yourself up for success *before* you're in a position to make a decision. For example: you can set up a system with your bank so that they will automatically put a percentage or amount of your paycheck into your savings account. This forced savings adds up over time, and the precommitment makes it much easier to stick to a good decision.

It also makes it *harder* to make the wrong decision.

It's shocking how much we will do simply because we're lazy. Try and make as many decisions as you can when you're already in a motivated state—this way, the pressure's off in the moment. Then, if you feel tempted to slack off, it'll take more effort to undo the good decision you made earlier. The pain of losing out on money for a workout class you won't attend might just help you get up and get it done.

Make it fun

One habit that I'm working on right now is using an actual alarm clock instead of my phone. In theory, using my phone isn't a problem—but when I wake up and my phone is next to me, I *rarely* get right out of bed. Social media, checking my email, and replying to texts grab my attention, and before long, I've wasted an hour of my life.

This is something I've been wanting to do for a while, and in a moment of inspiration, I bought a digital alarm clock off of Amazon that I love the look of. It replaces the needed functionality of my phone, and the fact that it fits the room and aesthetic so well actually makes it kind of fun for me to use.

Wherever you can, look for opportunities to make habits *enjoyable*. Don't base your ability to be consistent on it, but get creative. Finding little ways to make otherwise mundane habits more exciting or enticing can help a lot, especially in the beginning. That whole enthusiast thing comes in handy here—get stoked about what you're doing and why it's benefiting you, even if in the moment, it's not what you want to be spending your time on.

If you ask me, the idea that personal growth has to be painful in order to be effective is a myth. "No pain, no gain" has been overly romanticized to leave us with the expectation that if something doesn't hurt, it's not working.

Growth is rarely comfortable. By definition, to learn, you must step at least partly into the unknown, but it doesn't have to hurt. In fact, with this mentality, you're likely to end up working against yourself and making things much harder than they need to be.

Be your own ally. Do yourself a favour, and look for

ways to make habit building and growth *fun*. In the early stages, it's a helpful boost, but in the long run, enjoying the process will help you stay on track.

Make it real

When you picture the future you, you're probably pretty great. You can see yourself hitting all your goals, nailing all the habits you want to build, and perfecting what you currently struggle to accomplish.

But the more ideal a vision, the less motivation there is to risk it.

Meaning—you may never get started.

Working towards something makes it real, and making it real means there's a chance that it won't go the way you want it to. And honestly, that doesn't usually motivate you to take risks.

I thought about writing this book for *years* before I started. In my head, it was perfect. I had a clear vision, I was eloquent and the thoughts I had simply tumbled off of the page. Everyone reading it was touched, and it went exactly how I always dreamed it would. But the unattainability of that dream made it very, very difficult to actually get started.

I don't know about you, but time and time again, I find myself dreaming up all of the positive changes I'm going to make in my life. The new project I'll start next week, the leap I'll take next month. But dreaming about it doesn't necessarily lead me to jump right in.

A great way to make something real is to write it down.

Actually writing something down increases its likelihood of happening. It makes it feel real, and it becomes harder to avoid. Even if writing it down is all you've done, there is some sense of accountability.

It's partly because of this that I have found so much value in a daily planner. Physically writing down and scheduling the habits I want to practice means that I know when and where I'm supposed to do them. I'm looking at the list all day, and it's pretty hard to forget. If I want to ignore them, I have to consciously choose to use that time for something else.

Make it simple

While I'm hoping you're feeling inspired, motivated, and eager to jump into this new way of life, I would suggest working on no more than three habits at once. It's far too easy to bite off more than you can chew, and feeling like a failure is not conducive to a motivated life.

As different opportunities come up, look for chances to build any habits you want to—but go slowly, and prioritize one at a time. *Working up* to the life you want is much more effective than trying to force it. Long-term results > instant satisfaction.

In *Atomic Habits,* James Clear proposes this idea of the "2-minute habit strategy"[2]. He argues that a new habit should take you no longer than 2 minutes to complete. If the thing you're working towards takes longer than that, break it down, and find a 2-minute long version to start with.

If you want to clean your kitchen every night, a 2-minute habit could look like loading the dishwasher.

Starting a journaling practice might look like writing down one word every day to represent something that you're grateful for.

Two minutes or less, Clear suggests, is the best way to ensure that you can and will keep coming back to something. The commitment is short enough that it's harder to talk yourself out of, and much more difficult to avoid.

After that first two-minute habit becomes easy—a staple part of your routine - add on to it with the next two-minute habit. Cleaning the kitchen extends to loading the dishwasher *and* wiping down the counters, or writing down five things that you're grateful for instead of one.

The 4-minute rule

A couple of years ago, I began implementing something called the "4-minute rule".

The 4-minute rule isn't specifically related to goal setting, but I think it's appropriate to insert here. The idea is simple. Every time you enter a new space throughout your day, whether it's waking up in the morning, stepping into class, or heading into a meeting, spend the first four minutes focused solely on being the *absolute best version* of yourself.

For just 4 minutes.

Be friendly and put a smile on your face. Walk into a class or meeting expecting it to be productive and willing to contribute. When you meet up with friends, ask more questions than you give statements and focus on listening to them.

Those 4 minutes fly by before you know it. Now, of course, the goal here isn't really about those 4 minutes—it's that over time, you stop thinking about the minutes and those actions just become your normal. I can personally attest to the difference that this has made in my life.

I don't even think about the timing anymore, except on the rare occasion that I'm in an extraordinarily bad mood. In this case, I do focus on those 4 minutes. I try and think of things that I'm thankful for, look for opportunities to boost my mood, and shift my view to be more reflective and grateful.

I don't *have* to go to school today, I *get* to receive an education.

I don't *have* to grab coffee with someone I don't feel like seeing today, I *get* to encourage someone else.

When those 4 minutes are up, I feel lighter. My actions, thoughts, and beliefs have usually shifted. The 4-minute rule is a habit that's designed to disappear on its own— a practice that transforms every part of your being and, when it's no longer needed, it fades away.

Maybe you can't become your best self overnight, but you *can* be better for just 4 minutes.

Keep goals in their lane

One very, very important thing that you need to know about goal setting - it's not everything. Hitting your targets is great, but it's not worth killing yourself over. Goals can be an instrumental part of your development, or they can be something minor that you play around with and decide isn't for you.

Don't get me wrong, I think goal setting is incredibly powerful - and it's skyrocketed my growth as an individual and as a writer. But I've also had to learn how to manage them. Assigning goals a proper value and keeping them in their lane has been instrumental for healthy self-esteem.

Goal-oriented personality types may thrive when they have something to work towards, but they can also forget to stop and breathe. Your goals are not the answer or secret to your happiness. Hitting them has no effect on your value and you don't have to earn anything. They are a target, something to work towards, but they should also be flexible. Life gets crazy, and you can't possibly plan for everything that's to come.

Do not let your happiness or self-worth depend on hitting a target this month.

Time is too precious and goes by too quickly to obsess or micromanage. No matter what, don't stop having fun, living life, and enjoying the things around you. Goals are a means to an end. *They are not the end themselves.*

CHAPTER FIVE:
Habits

Three years ago, I stumbled onto a YouTube video[1] from a former Google design ethicist on the addictive nature of smartphones.

The short video broke down some of the incredibly simple ways that our devices are built and designed to hook us permanently. From the unpredictable nature of notifications—will they be positive, negative, when will they show up—to the exact colours used in alert messages, it's no wonder they steal so much of our time.

Some phone features, like the "pull to refresh" on Twitter or Instagram are even made to mimic slot machines, creating powerful addictions that have become normalized to most of us. If we spent as much time doing anything else as we do on our smartphones, there would be alarm bells going off.

Cell phones, however, have become an indispensable part of the daily routine. In such a short time, our means of communication, relationship to technology, and method of accessing information have shifted entirely.

As I reflected on my relationship to my phone, I realized that the habits I had developed weren't ones I was proud of. Over the next few days, I spent a lot of time thinking about what it would look like to cut back on my screen time. Eventually, I decided that it had to be done. I was missing out on life, getting caught up in social media, and was addicted to things I didn't even care about.

I went through my apps, deleted ones I didn't use or want, and changed my phone settings so that my screen was in grayscale. I was passionately committed to this new shift in my life, and eager to talk about it.

This was a new chapter for me. I was motivated, excited, and passionate about this change.

But after years of nonstop smartphone usage, the habits weren't that easy to break.

Reaching for my phone happened without me even thinking about it. I had deleted time-sucking apps, but my muscle memory still tapped the empty space on the screen where they had been before. The grayscale definitely made the experience less satisfying, but all I had to do to turn it off was to click my power button three times—something which also became a habit.

I *wanted* to change, but it was like my brain didn't

get the memo. I felt helpless and guilty, confused and conflicted over how to change my habits. Eventually, I gave up.

Smartphone usage isn't the only time I've had that experience. Breaking longstanding habits is a lot harder than it sounds.

The importance of habits

On a daily basis, up to almost *half* of everything you do is habitual. From the moment you wake up, your automated behaviours carry you through all your regular tasks: checking your phone, getting out of bed, taking a shower, driving a car.

Unconscious habits like opening up Instagram, reaching for a cigarette, or taking a sip of water may appear small and inconsequential on their own. But collectively, your little habits make up most of your life and who you are. These habits decide what kind of worker you are, what kind of parent and friend. They shape what your free time looks like, how you show up for other people, and impact your health in every sense.

It's for this reason that the narratives "Willpower is everything" or "Motivation above all else" simply don't hold up.

Feeling motivated is great, but it's not something you can always control. On its own, inspiration won't catapult you to where you want to be. Your habits don't change just because you want them to.

There's not enough inspirational quotes in the world to undo a lifetime of bad habits.

Author and habit expert James Clear wrote, "Bad habits repeat themselves again and again not because you don't want to change, but because you have the wrong system for change."[2]

While moving forward in life is impossible without knowing where you want to go, getting there will be a constant uphill battle without habits as a key part of your strategy.

Changing your habits is the easiest way to get where you want to go. It's also the best way to become the person that you want to be. Intentional habit-building goes beyond a general vision of what you're working towards.

It looks at the little moments—the things you do when no one is watching. The character you display, the quality of life you experience, and the movements and decisions that you make in the dark.

We typically think of who we are now as very different from the person we will be in the future, so consider how your future self will act.

What habits will you have?

When you come home from work, how will you spend your evenings?

What will your morning routine look like?

Who are the people that you will spend the most time with, and what do you contribute to those relationships?

Living life on purpose isn't just about changing your external direction. The best way to work towards your goals in any category—relationships, career, financial or otherwise—is to prioritize becoming the kind of person that succeeds in those areas.

In order to have the kind of relationship you want, you need to become the kind of partner you want to be. Getting your dream job won't do you much good if you haven't developed the necessary skills to do it well. All the money in the world won't teach you how to budget if you can't manage less.

We tend to expect that when we get where we want to go, our circumstances will make us into the person we want to be, but it's usually the opposite.

It is far more likely that who you are will change your reality than that your reality will change who you are.

There's this Biblical principle in the book of Luke that explains this well (yes, this is relevant even if you're not a Christian, I promise). The ESV translation for Luke 16:10 says this: "One who is faithful in a very little is also faithful in much, and one who is dishonest in a very little is also dishonest in much."[3]

In this context, Jesus is specifically talking about money—making the point that how much you have of something doesn't change your integrity or character. Those who are wise and faithful when they have only a little of something will also be so when they have a lot.

But if you don't learn to handle what you have, well, what makes you think you could handle *more* better?

It's something that's stuck with me, and I think the principle applies to a lot more than just money. If you were to wake up tomorrow morning in your dream job, having won the lottery, or just about to meet "the one"—you would still be exactly the same person that you are now.

Philosopher Will Durant, in referencing the teachings of Aristotle, wrote "We are what we repeatedly do. Excellence, then, is not an act, but a habit."[4]

Maybe the only thing holding you back from where you want to be is your circumstances. Maybe not. But it's worth considering the ways in which you can prepare yourself for whatever lies ahead.

Who you are is not defined so much by your conscious decisions as by your habits, your often unconscious repeated behaviours. They shape who you are becoming, how you respond to situations, and a lot of what your future will look like.

The habits you have right now are directing your steps, whether you know it or not.

But while you can't change the automated nature of your brain's programming, you can decide to take the reins for yourself. Rather than waiting to see where your unconscious mind is leading you, you can build habits intentionally.

Those ideal habits that your future self has? Start implementing them now. The only way you're going to get from Point A to Point B is if you actually start moving.

Habits compound over time, meaning that the more you repeat an action, the easier it becomes. The sooner you start integrating your desired habits into your everyday life, the sooner they become a part of you.

Your habits are a prediction of your future, but they're not set in stone. They can be shifted, altered, and redirected. Building new pathways in your brain allows you to redefine what your everyday life looks like.

Knowing what matters to you is the foundation for an intentional life, habit-building is the framework.

Habits are the structure that everything else gets built around. It's your little things adding up, your small choices making big impacts, and your future changing around you.

In order to start the process of habit-building, you first need to understand how and why the brain builds habits—something writer Charles Duhigg dubbed "the habit loop."[5]

The Habit Loop

The human brain is an incredible thing. Between keeping you alive, running your life, and maintaining what sometimes feels like a never-ending to-do list, it doesn't always get enough credit.

Even the act of habit-building is an incredible feat. The brain is, essentially, the ultimate environmentalist. It conserves energy like nothing else. Your brain makes up roughly 2% of your weight,[6] but it accounts for 20% of the energy you use in a day,[7] and if it wasn't for habits, that second number would be a lot higher.

Because the brain is constantly burning energy, it has a system. It automates *everything* that it possibly can. The less you're thinking about what you do, the easier it is to do it. When something is automatic, or at least regular, it takes a lot less energy than it does the first couple of times you do it.

Basically, your brain keeps track of everything

you do and looks for repeating tasks. When you do something over and over, a neural pathway is formed. The more you do it, the stronger the pathway becomes.

Habits become faster and easier, instinctive and normal. Tying your shoes, driving a car, and brushing your teeth were all once new and exhausting, but at a certain point, they probably became automatic.

The power of habit in your life is hard to understate. It begins from the moment you are born and will continue until the day you die. But for every bad habit, accidental routine, or loop you no longer want in your life, there's an opportunity to create new patterns.

Leveraging the impact of habit is quite simple, and it's easily the most effective way to create lasting behaviour change. The more you do something, the more it becomes a part of you.

The best way to start the process of leveraging your habits is to simply pay attention.

Start noticing what you do in a day, from the moment you get up to when your head hits the pillow. Don't guilt-trip or critique yourself, just notice. Look at what you do, what you want to do, and what feels normal.

If you're up to the task, grab a notebook and record

an actual "habit inventory" for a week or two. Keep a record of what you do with no guilt, criticism, or feelings attached. The goal is not to be a better version of yourself during this time, but simply to track your habitual behaviour and get a sense of where you're actually at.

In the wise words of my favourite reality TV guru, Dr. Phil, "You can't change what you don't acknowledge."

You need to know what's *there* in order to know what it means to you, and in all likelihood, you probably have a lot of great habits that you'll want to keep.

Understanding your habits and where they come from begins by examining them through the lens of the habit loop. Every expert, researcher, and author seems to come up with their own names for these steps, but the process is the same. First, a cue or craving initiates the behaviour or routine, and immediately after comes a reward.

Cue

A habit cue is a signal to your brain that it's time for a specific action. This could be a rising sense of stress, arriving home from work, or seeing Starbucks on your way into the office. It's also referred to as a craving. This cue is what prompts you to act. It'd the thing that triggers a desire or instinctual move. If you've ever taken a psychology class, you know that classical conditioning is more or less the process of creating a cue.

Identifying the cues behind your habits is the first step to shifting them. For every behaviour, positive, negative, or otherwise, there is a prompt telling you to do so.

You grab your phone from beside your bed because your alarm went off and you don't want to get up.

You brush your teeth because your mouth tastes bad in the morning.

You fill up your gas tank because the light came on.

You order food because you're hungry.

You start making coffee because you feel tired.

The cues are what trigger your brain to move. They're instinctive. In all likelihood, they're so ingrained in your life and mind that you probably don't notice when they happen. A cue prompts a quick response, and it's then that you move into the actual habitual behaviour.

Routine

This is your habit. It's the act of brushing your teeth, filling up your gas tank, or grinding coffee beans with your eyes still half-closed from sleep.

It's something that you do over and over, whether you know it or not. Checking your phone, buying lunch out, calling your mom while you run errands. Whatever habits look like in your life, this is them.

The term "habit" is often associated with negative things—biting your fingernails, sleeping in too late, forgetting to take the meat out of the freezer. But all it really means is something consistent.

Filling up your water bottle is a habit. Telling your significant other that you love them is a habit. Eating healthy foods (or not) is a habit. All of the things that you do on a regular basis are habits.

As you create your habit inventory and notice the little things that you do, take some time to stop and see if you can identify what your cues may be.

A cue is usually not a negative thing, it's simply a need or deep want. Your behaviour is your attempt to satisfy it, and that's where things get tricky. Sometimes the ways in which we try to meet our own needs aren't the most effective.

Understanding where your behaviours come from and what is actually prompting them will make it *much* easier for you to change, break, or create new rhythms.

Reward

The reward is the final part of the habit loop. This is when your brain gets a little boost of happiness. It's what solidifies something as a behaviour that you want to repeat.

You get a hit of serotonin when you see your message notifications, a release of endorphins from a workout, or experience the energy boost from caffeine hitting your system.

It can be an external reward, too. Maybe your boss compliments you on your work every time you ask him how his weekend was. Your significant other gives you more affection when you tell them you've had a rough day. Your coworker offers you a mint every time you restart your computer.

It can be as simple as a feel-good moment or as significant as a paycheck hitting the bank. Your reward keeps you coming back, and it's a powerful incentive. It tells your brain "We like this," and so your brain adds it into automated behaviours.

The habit loop is wired into every part of your life. From what you eat, to how you spend your time, to the kind of friend, partner, and worker you are.

Understanding it empowers you to see your actions differently. When you're aware of the role habits play in your life, you actually have the power to choose what you want to make consistent rather than simply letting it choose you.

Breaking the cycle

When it comes to breaking bad habits, the best place to start is to study the cue. Let's say you want to stop buying lunch out every day. Buying lunch isn't inherently "bad", but depending on your financial situation, it may not be helpful.

First things first —what's the cue?

Probably hunger. You need to eat, and when your body starts sending you signals that it's time, you want to satisfy your craving. Most cues on their own aren't good or bad at all—they're just parts of life. You need to eat to live, and on a basic level, that's what your body is asking for.

Rather than trying to eliminate your craving, find a different, better way to satisfy it.

I'm using this example in part because it's similar to one of the habits that I had a very hard time shifting when I first began the process of intentional living. At the time, I was a full-time student and ate out a lot. I knew it wasn't the best financial option, but honestly, I didn't have the time or energy to prepare lunch every evening.

But I hit some financial roadblocks, and things had to change. For a while, I stopped eating lunch altogether, which was a very, very bad solution.

It was through this dilemma that I discovered the art of meal prepping. Once a week, on a weekend morning I would sit down and pick 3-4 meals that I wanted to cook for the week. I made sure that they were ones that I could eat over and over.

I made *one* trip to the grocery store, list in hand, and bought only the things that I needed for that week. I came home, and almost immediately, made them all at once, while I still felt motivated. I only invested a couple of hours, but when I was done, I had lunch and dinners for the week. I saved an insane amount of money, ate a lot healthier, and didn't even have to think about what I would eat most days.

That was years ago, and I still try to meal prep every week. If you want to try meal prepping, you can find more resources at *outofthehabit.com* and download a free printable meal planner at *outofthehabit.com/printable-meal-planner/*.

The cue wasn't a problem, and the reward wasn't either. The habit was based on a real and healthy need, I just had to find a better way to meet it.

Similarly, you can resolve boredom by going for a run rather than playing a game on your phone or reading a book rather than watching TV. Avoid spending money on grabbing coffee in the mornings by getting a machine that you can set up and program the night before.

Craving stimulation might lead you to a video game, stress might lead you to smoke or drink, and loneliness might tempt you to call your ex—but giving yourself different alternatives, especially ones you plan ahead, can help break the habit.

Similar to goal setting, one of the best ways to invest in your habits is to *pre-commit yourself* to better decisions. Doing the healthier thing *in advance* sets you up for success when you're in moments of temptation. For example: deleting someone's number *before* you get the urge to call them. Meal prepping for the week ahead *before* you want to buy lunch. Setting up your bank account with auto-savings *before* the money actually hits.

That said, "breaking bad habits" is kind of a myth. Longstanding neural pathways have strong, thick connections that will be impossible to just sever. It doesn't matter how much willpower you have, your brain and body are used to doing things a certain way. Instead of emphasizing avoidance, focus on creating new pathways— ones that will solve problems and satisfy cravings in healthier ways.

Timing

It's not all hype—making changes during a natural period of transition is actually ideal. When you change jobs, move to a new location, or flip the calendar page, you are accepting the message that something new is beginning. Psychologically speaking, you'll have a much easier time making lasting change in your life if it also coincides with a change in your environment.

There actually *is* something to be said for New Years Resolutions. A boost of inspiration or motivation won't change your life all by itself, but the push can be really valuable. That does *not* mean you should wait until the end of the year to make a change, but even starting something new at the beginning of a week or month is likely to help you out.[8]

Time and time again, people have found it easier to change or eliminate habits in new settings. Going on vacation, changing your environment—even moving around your furniture can help. That little environmental shift helps you see the potential for change. During these times, it's actually more feasible for us to accept that we can change as well.

Visual cues

Visual cues are also a really helpful tool, as they can trigger habits in and of themselves. A remote sitting out might prompt you to turn on the TV. Laying out your workout clothes in the morning can give you a nudge to hit the gym when you get home. These simple triggers are quite effective, and for better or worse, it's a good thing to be aware of.

If you're trying to break or change a habit, consider whether there are any visual cues that may make that harder. Getting rid of the cues can, on occasion, even eliminate habits altogether. If you are no longer reminded of the craving, you probably won't repeat the action.

In the same way that your environment and atmosphere can trigger habits that you don't want, it can just as easily cue habits that you do. If you don't want to sleep with your phone in your room, put your charger in the kitchen. If you want to start running, leave your shoes out where you can see them.

Making healthy snacks more visible and accessible makes it more likely that you'll reach for them.

Consider the people that you spend time with. Are these people who will encourage your growth and call you to be better? Or are they people who will try to pull you into old habits because it's what they know and enjoy?

We're all on our own path, and you don't necessarily have to cut people off who have different priorities. But in the early stages of growth and development, it's certainly worth paying attention to the impact that different people have on your life.

The truth about "bad" habits

Something to keep in mind through this process is that your bad habits may not actually be bad at all. In fact, the cues that prompt them are probably completely normal. Your feelings and cravings are likely no different than anyone else's. You just need a healthy strategy for how to fulfill them.

Focus on shifting your habits, rather than eliminating them.

This is a highly effective strategy, particularly if you're your own worst critic. When you see your craving as synonymous with negative patterns, it can be tempting to just try and rid yourself of the desire altogether. This is a much harder task, and it may not be necessary.

If biting your nails is a stress behaviour for you, the problem isn't biting your nails, it's that you need a better way to cope with stress. The habit is a temporary fix, and not a good one.

Separating the craving from the behaviour can help you find better strategies to discover what you actually need. Be your own friend, not an enemy.

As you work to shift negative behaviours, it's important to prioritize developing positive habits.

Habits and who you want to be

As is the case with any intentional growth, healthy habit building begins by figuring out who you want to be and working backwards. The person you are becoming does not, will not, and cannot simply appear. They are forged in the fire. Built from little moments. They exist because they are you, choosing to change your everyday rhythms and behaviours. Breaking down the overarching vision for your life into smaller, actionable pieces.

Of course, not all habits are bad, and you probably want to keep some of the ones you have. Even objectively "good" habits aren't universal—your life and goals are different from everyone else's, and your lives will look different because of it.

The truth is, though, that the person that you want to be in the future likely has *different* everyday habits than you do right now.

Habit formation isn't complicated, but rebuilding neural pathways does take time. When you're changing the way that you've responded to something over a long period, maybe even the majority of your life, it's a process. For something to become an automatic, repeated behaviour, it must first become a regular part of your life.

Habits and Priorities

Where a habit inventory assesses the habits that you already have, this step is about reflecting on the habits you *want* to have. The behaviours and decisions that you would like to be instinctive and automatic.

The little moments of our lives define us more than we would like to think. It's actually easier sometimes to be your ideal self in the big ones—when you're aware of the significance of your actions.

But getting up in the morning doesn't feel like a big deal. What you eat today doesn't feel like it has anything to do with the trajectory of your life. Even the way you treat or respond to your partner in a given situation may seem small or unimportant.

And on their own, each of these things is relatively small. When you repeat them, however, when they become habits and patterns in your everyday life, that's a very different conversation.

You're not just laying in bed for an extra 10 minutes one morning—you are consistently starting your days with procrastination. You're not just treating yourself here and there, you're eating a diet that can have severely negative consequences on your long-term health. It's not that you forgot about date night this one time, it's that you often do, communicating to your partner that they're not a priority.

All of these behaviours *can* be one-offs. Doing something once doesn't make it a habit. But if these things are natural or even instinctive to you, and you're not consciously doing something else, they will likely become automatic over time.

So in order to become the person that you want to be, building good and healthy habits is essential.

Building healthy habits
1. Start somewhere

Habit building is a process, but you have to start somewhere. Look for an opportunity to brainstorm the specific habits you'd like to have at some point in your life. Start as general as you'd like (again, working backwards can be really helpful) and get as detailed as possible.

Think about your routines, relationships, health, and hobbies. What would you like an average day or week to look like in your life, and what would you need to change to make that happen?

Here are some prompts to help get you thinking:

1. What is your ideal morning routine?
2. How does the best version of you take care of your health?
3. What hobbies would you like to develop?
4. What qualities do you want to demonstrate as a friend, and how can you do that better?
5. What do you want to exhibit every day as a partner or spouse?

Some of my own habit goals have included:

1. I want a balanced diet. I want to eat mostly healthy but feel okay having treats too.
2. I want a creative hobby, like painting. Something that's not a side hustle or for profit, but that's purely fun for me.
3. When I'm out and I notice something nice about someone, I want to actually tell that person. (Ex. "That's a cute shirt"/dog/etc.)

These habits are different from other goals in that they aren't things you "hit" or accomplish—they're things that you become. This is your starting point. Your habits make you, shape you, and affect every interaction and relationship that you have. They don't just get you to a certain point, they keep you in a state of being and growing.

2. Prioritize

Next, it's time to prioritize—to *intentionally* select which habits are most important or most relevant to your life right now. Doing too much at once will lead you to overwhelm, then burnout. You can't get anywhere if you push too hard.

The goal of behaviour change isn't to alter everything, or really anything overnight. Not only is this impossible, but it's not *real*. Too far, too fast, is only setting yourself up to fail.

And here's the thing—goals, intentionality, habit building—all of those things will end up changing your external circumstances. But they'll do far more for who you are as a person.

The real way that you create a life you love isn't by filling it with everything you want, but by becoming someone who knows how to love life.

It's worth considering, too, what it would look like to be that version of yourself in the circumstance that you're in.

We often think of the person we want to be as someone living an entirely different life. Their homes are bigger, their stuff is nicer—they might even look different. Their friendships, relationships and career are *better* and *fuller* but what would it look like to simply be a better version of you right where you are?

If you were the person that you want to be in the future *right now,* how would that change your life?

In fact, what if *nothing* in your circumstance changed except your mindset?

This is the true goal of intentional living. Crafting a life that you love, but not through money or certificates or other people's approval. Living out your priorities often has a way of getting you where you want to go, but it changes you first.

When you go to set goals, implement habits, or prioritize behaviour change, keep in mind *what matters most* through every stage. Your priorities, big goals, and values in life will help you take things one step at a time and make sure you are always becoming the person you want to be.

Habit stacking

Social scientist BJ Fogg proposed a fascinating technique for habit-building a few years ago. "Habit stacking" is the act of inserting habits that you want to build into already-established routines.[9] Things like brushing your teeth, putting on your shoes, and eating lunch are all established routines. You do them every day, and they're not going anywhere.

Practicing habit stacking simply means tucking

something into the middle or onto the end of a routine. For example, immediately after you finish brushing your teeth, you grab your gratitude journal and sit down to write, or, as you put on your work shoes to leave for the day, review your top priorities and goals before you ever set foot in the office.

Think about the habit loop: cue, routine, reward. You may know the routine you want to build, but what's your cue? What's your reward? It might be a sudden feeling of happiness, a more productive day. Maybe it's the satisfying feeling of crossing it off in your planner.

Above all, in building new habits, focus on consistency over perfection. Repetition is the goal here. Your "form" is not top priority in the beginning. It's worth doing things right as much as possible—you don't want to build the wrong habit—but if you only complete an action when it's perfect, you won't build a habit at all.

Going 110% is great—but if you need to half-ass it sometimes, be at peace with that. You are human, you have limitations, and that's okay.

Perfection is the enemy of growth.

Even greatness, let alone perfection, is not an accident. In order to do something well, you need to be willing to first learn to do it poorly. Over time, you can develop skill and technique, but Rome wasn't built in a day.

While there is no singular action, choice or mistake that defines you, your habits are as close as they come. The things that you do on a daily or near-daily basis, over and over, without even thinking start to become part of you.

As you go through this process, remember to be kind to yourself.

Self-criticism is not a good form of motivation.

Rather than encouraging you to work harder, it often makes giving up seem more and more attractive.

Don't.

Just because you haven't succeeded in an area before doesn't mean that you can't now. When you hear stories of success, people tell you about how good it felt to get a breakthrough, or how much they hustled to get there. They don't tell you that it took them years of failing and recalibrating and looking at things differently before they discovered the real principles of behaviour change.

Habits are powerful and can be shifted and developed. Anyone who's ever said "People can't change" didn't do enough research. It takes time, commitment, and a willingness to learn, but your habits are malleable.

The things you have done in the past are in the past, and the things you are doing, positive or negative, are not the end of your potential. Stay the path, don't rush it, and remain fixed on what you're actually working towards. Your habits are the *first step* to developing deep, lasting, permanent change, not the end of the road.

CHAPTER SIX:
Know Yourself

Why you matter

"Knowing yourself is the beginning of all wisdom."

Aristotle

At the time I'm writing this, the global population is exactly 7,886,872,950. The world is filled with people, each with their own story, personality, and genetic makeup. We have our own goals, ideas, beliefs and perspectives on everything around us, so much so that at times it feels as if our uniqueness is the only thing we have in common.

Even if every person on the planet were to put intentional living into action, none of that would change. I think the world would be better, and that people would generally feel happier with more productive attitudes, but our lives would still look different from each others'.

The thing about intentional living is that it doesn't tell you what to work for, what goals to set, or who you should be. Those things are distinctive to you and you alone. What intentional living does is help you *get* there. This way of life prepares you for whatever is coming your way, using your own strengths, some strategy, and purposeful action.

Success isn't just about working hard. Determination is part of it, but you can work hard and still go in circles all day.

The idea of "working smart" isn't just a motivational cliche—it's a lifesaving strategy. When you understand that your natural resources—your energy, emotional capacity, and time - are limited, you invest them differently. But while this is universally true, it looks different for everyone.

Direction is what gives purpose to your action. It creates a destination for your efforts, a target and intent and an aim to work towards. But it's more than an outlet, it's the guiding force behind getting from where you are now to where you want to end up.

Knowing your priorities and values in life is an invaluable beginning. But it's not enough to just know these things—you also need to know *yourself*.

On a physical level, you are made up of bones, muscle, tissue, blood, and a whole host of other things. This, you *do* share in common with the people around you. But you are more than that, too.

Your genetic influences, life experience, and personality are all part of who you are. Nature *and* nurture. *This* is the you that you need to know. Our habits and behaviours are often symptoms of our internalized beliefs, and changing them will only do so much if we don't address how they were formed.

What you believe about yourself is directly tied to *what you do*. To alter one and not the other is almost impossible.

According to psychologist Tasha Eurich, 95% of people think they're self-aware. But her research has shown that only 10-15% of people *actually are.1*

Statistically speaking, you probably don't know yourself as well as you think you do. Which makes getting to the root of what you want out of life all the more difficult. The good news is that self-awareness isn't fixed. It can actually be cultivated and developed over time.

Knowing yourself comes from reflection. It means being honest about your strengths, weaknesses, pain points and history. The good, the bad, and anything in between. A healthy self-awareness is often most obvious in hard moments. Being able to recognize when you've screwed up and how is invaluable, but not universal—not everyone can do it.

Without self-awareness, you will likely struggle to

build lasting, healthy relationships, find what really matters, and completely heal from what you've walked through. But with it, you'll gain greater insight into what makes you who you are and what makes you tick.

Consciously breaking down what matters, examining your habits, and focusing on what makes you happy all help you get to know yourself. But it's more than that. Getting to the root of where you are, who you are and how you got there gives you a more complete picture.

You matter. To other people and to the world, but also to yourself, whether you feel it or not. Self-understanding is different from self-care in that it's not about feeling good or getting rest. It's a form of respect.

Self-understanding acknowledges the truth and embraces it, which is a step you *have* to take before you can honestly move forward into anything more. We all have blind spots, but we have the option to shrink them by practicing and learning self-awareness.

Understanding where you're at and what's brought you here will help you build more successful habits, set more honest goals, and improve the quality of every relationship, job, and opportunity you have in life. You'll be a better communicator, a more competent adult, and far more prepared to take on whatever life throws at you.

On the other hand, a lack of self-awareness can be dangerous. Limiting beliefs are a thing, and they often slip by undetected. Self-sabotage is more common than you might think. We have a knack for getting in our own way - overcomplicating decisions, messing with what's right in front of us, and screwing up the things that we truly want.

But this isn't just about fixing negative habits. Being self-aware equips you to do **better** at pretty much everything. Realizing what motivates you and pushes you will help you accomplish any of your goals.

I have a theory about successful people. It's not that they all come from successful backgrounds or that they alone know how to work hard. I don't think they all went to the right university, heard the right TED talk, or that the universe dropped achievement in their lap.

My theory is that a significant portion of them either a) figured out what motivated them and leveraged it, or b) got lucky and just happened to find themselves in an environment that was perfect for their personality.

That's not to discredit hard work, skill, or determination, but wanting it "bad enough" doesn't get you there on its own. Environment plays a huge role, as does your mindset. Self-awareness is getting out of your own way, but it's also setting yourself up for success. Building systems, habits, and boundaries to create a life where you can thrive.

Who you are
What's Your Type?

When it comes to understanding and knowing yourself, personality is a great place to start. Coming to terms with the categories and terms which can explain certain parts of your person and life—things like extroversion vs. introversion—can be extremely helpful.

If you know that being with people too much is draining for you, you can keep that in mind when considering a career path, weekly schedule, and hobbies. This doesn't mean that you *can't* spend time with people, just that you'll want to create opportunities to be alone, too.

If you tend to be a logically-minded person, rather than an emotional one, you could come across as cold or unsympathetic without even thinking about it. Being aware of it, however, makes it easier for you to think through a situation before acting and considering how best to respond.

I want to preface this by saying that I am a big proponent of personality tests. I've taken many, some of which were incredibly valuable and others less so, but all of them helped me put together different pieces of who I am.

In my opinion, they're also *extremely* overvalued.

Here's the thing—personality tests, especially ones you give to yourself, are not as objective as they claim. When they're self-administered, you're not answering questions about who you are, but about who you *think* you are. Objectivity is not something we are entirely capable of, even if we are as honest as we can possibly be. (Remember that average self-awareness rate?)

It's impossible for you to *fully* see yourself as the person that you actually are, and when you take a personality test, that influences the outcome.

That said, they can be very helpful. Between breaking down instincts, habits, and emotional needs, personality tests can actually identify some really key factors of your person.

The Enneagram

According to the Enneagram Institute,[2] the Enneagram personality test is made up of 9 different personality types. The belief is that we are all born with one of these basic personality types. The Enneagram is extremely popular and for many, it's been life changing. (I recently heard it referred to as the "Christian horoscope", though it's not religious-based.)

There are tons of books, podcasts, and resources for those looking to find out more about their

Enneagram type and what it means. To take the test and find out more information, visit ***enneagramin-stitute.com.***

Myers-Briggs

The Myers-Briggs personality test, or MBTI, is based on the work of Carl Jung. It looks at four components of personality: extraversion/introversion, thinking/feeling, judging/perceiving, and sensing/intuiting. Each person is assigned a letter from one of the two categories from the test, and ends up with a combination of four that provides them with basic information about their own personality and tendencies.

To take the MBTI, visit ***myersbriggs.org.***

One of the biggest perks of personality tests is that they are ***great*** at helping you identify certain career options and rule out others. They help identify categorical, label-able traits that clarify both good options and fits that are less than ideal.

Personality tests may reveal how your environment affects you, what you are like in social situations, and where you thrive in your everyday life. Imagine a world where every time you set a goal, you knew how to do it in the way that made the most sense for you. This is a ***gamechanger*** for anyone trying to create change.

Your relationships to conflict, planning, stressors and stress behaviours are often entirely unconscious—and a lack of awareness of this can be detrimental. Personality tests are a great place to start asking questions and developing self-awareness.

I'm a planner by nature. I like knowing what's ahead of me, both in work and in life. I *thrive* on to-do lists. If something matters to me, I want it booked, written down, and put in my Google Calendar. I know myself and my habits, and I know that if I don't plan it and make it a priority, it won't happen. I plan things *because* they matter to me.

My boyfriend, on the other hand, is the opposite. He loves to be spontaneous, make last-minute plans, and go with the flow. When we first started dating, it used to drive me insane. Based on the way that I'm wired, I interpreted it as a lack of caring or commitment that he didn't want to plan our date nights three months in advance (okay, I'm exaggerating a little). This is probably the biggest difference in our personalities, and in the beginning, it was really hard.

After recognizing that this was a difference in wiring, and *not* in commitment, things got a lot better. Without that understanding, however, I would've gone on feeling less and less important for no reason.

Knowing your personality types and tendencies makes everything easier. Work communication, conflict, making friends and applying for jobs all become smoother processes when you know what's good for you and what isn't.

Information & Identity

Aside from the lack of objectivity, personality tests aren't *all* beneficial. In fact, they can actually be quite harmful when used in the wrong way.

Learning about your personality type is one thing.

Making it your identity is another.

All too often, the results of a personality test become a set of limitations. They're assumed to be a defined future, list of boundaries, and lines you shouldn't bother trying to cross. They become an excuse for bad habits, an explanation for mistakes, and a central part of how you see yourself.

The problem with this is that *you are not your personality.* Your identity is so much more, and seeing the results of a manmade test or quiz as capable of defining it is incredibly risky.

It's valuable information, to be sure. It might even explain some of your stress behaviours and choices. But to interpret it as a core tenet of your being is just inaccurate.

When they're misused or taken advantage of, personality types can become toxic and detrimental to your growth. They need to stay in their lane, and you need to remember that they are merely a loose assessment—a generic categorization of an entire person, life, and being. You could not possibly be defined or encapsulated in a generic, 30-question quiz.

Your personality might mean you're inclined to certain actions or behaviours, but it absolutely does *not* control you.

You are in charge of and responsible for the actions you take—those are on you.

To sum up—personality tests are a tool, and when used as such, are appropriate and healthy. They can provide beneficial insights, tips, and strategies with which to build a life you love. The information that they give you is not entirely objective, but it can lead to new information and revelations about who you are.

As you grow, you will be forever changing, forever becoming. The journey of knowing yourself is lifelong, but it is a wonderful one.

For every flaw, tendency, and habit you wish you never had, there is a heart, an instinct, and a desire that is making the world better. When you see both sides, you can choose which ones to cultivate and grow in your life. Take the information with a grain of salt, but take it. The parts you like and the parts that sting a little. Pay attention to what you hear, and decide what you want to do with it.

Self-sabotage: the unforeseen enemy

Almost every great story has a tale of betrayal. A well-loved character, a hero in the making, a valued team member who turns to the other side. Someone you never expected to be fighting against the good guys—but they can't seem to help it.

This is how I think of self-sabotage. It's the ultimate betrayal, to work against your conscious self, subtly destroying the things that you *think* you're working towards.

The majority of us don't *think* we have self-sabotaging tendencies. Why would we? It's bizarre to even suggest that **you** might be the thing keeping you from what you're working towards. It's also much easier to place blame outside of yourself.

And listen, you may be facing real roadblocks. But it's important to make sure that your mindset is in the right spot too.

Self-sabotage is when your thoughts, feelings and fears direct your actions in such a way that you almost cause your own failure. This is often entirely unconscious, and can be caused by feelings you don't even know you have.

It might look like always getting into relationships with the wrong people. Avoiding risk so you don't have to experience rejection. Massively overshooting so that you are in control of your success, or rather, lack of it. An all-or-nothing mindset is a self-sabotager's best friend.

You don't know what you don't know, which is why practicing self-awareness is *so* key. When it comes to self-sabotage, you will often be completely blind to the ways that you mess things up for yourself—*until you're not.* There's nothing more abrasive than getting smacked in the face by your own unconscious self.

The sooner you see them, the less power and damage they can do in your life.

How to recognize self-sabotaging patterns

By this point, I'm sure you've read the words "But what do you *really* want?" more than enough. I won't ask again, but what I *will* say is that it's worth asking yourself why you don't have it.

For some, there will be obvious explanations. If you're just starting your career, you won't have hit your ultimate goal. Your age and life experience may be keeping you from the kind of relationship that you want to develop. You are only responsible for your own actions, and yet other people's choices still affect your life greatly.

With that said, take an inventory of what you have done lately to invest in your ultimate goals.

Maybe there are areas where you're not pushing very hard, and others where you're pushing too hard. Are you settling for something that's not *really* what you want, or consciously choosing to accept less than what you'd like, instead of holding out for the thing that you are actually craving?

The problem with self-help culture

In the beginning of this book, I expressed to you that I did *not* want to write a cheesy self-help book, and this is why: self-help culture *sucks.* It just does. It's a ridiculously profitable, wildly successful, and sometimes extremely toxic industry that can prey on people's vulnerabilities and insecurities.

Of course, this is not true of the whole industry. As a consumer and creator of self-help content, I can attest to the real value that's there, and affirm the countless people who've dedicated their lives to helping others better theirs. I've been writing and working in the industry for a number of years, and have witnessed and benefitted from many experts (many of whom are listed in the "extra resources" page at the end of the book). But I've also seen the dark side of the industry. Cash grabs for unfulfilled promises and emotional manipulation.

Self-help culture and self-help content/consumers are *not* synonymous. This is an important distinction. Self-help consumers are usually people searching for genuine resources and growth, and much self-help content is available to help them do just that.

The problem with self-help *culture*—and why it's so

wildly successful—is that it starts with truth. It takes a look at some honest realities about human nature, personal struggles, and current cultural issues. A problematic self-help book will tell you what your problems are, find your pain points and meet you there, slap you with some inspirational words about how to fix everything in your life and, when it doesn't work, blame you for everything.

There's a lot of strategy in creating emotional highs. Manipulating people into feeling powerful, strong, and important—without actually giving them the tools to change anything.

There is no writer, psychologist, or expert in the world that can fix your life.

Even intentional living, while clearly something transformative, will not alter your human-ness, and without action, the principles are entirely meaningless.

Self-help addiction is a real thing. It's the idea that you just need one more book, one more course, one more motivational speech that leaves you thinking "Wow! That was *it* for me!" But then nothing changes. And so it's not.

So it must be the next one.

I have seen firsthand the destructive impact that this can have both in the lives of an individual and the people around them.

Wanting to better yourself, change your life, or do something differently is a great goal. But self-help addiction can be a form of self-sabotage, too.

If you really want something, take the time to make a plan for it. Consider what is actually the best way to get it done. When it comes to personal growth, going slow is not a bad thing. Taking the time to actually implement any real change will set you up for much greater success in the long run.

Creating new patterns

Self-sabotaging tendencies are habits like anything else. And like other habits, they need to be changed in the same way. But because they often flow out of such deep, unconscious beliefs, slipping by without our permission, changing the narrative is particularly important here.

It doesn't really matter what area of life you're looking at, your beliefs dictate your actions. If you want to change a habit, you need to change what you think about it.

Whether fear, anger, or other unresolved emotions are holding you back, take the time to process them. Journal, talk to a friend, go to therapy—do whatever you need to do to confront the beliefs that you're holding on to. You may be surprised at how effective it is to simply say things out loud.

As you work through what you're feeling, thinking, and processing about life, use the opportunity to decide what a healthy version of your unhealthy patterns *would* look like.

If you were completely healed of your trauma, had worked through whatever pain was affecting you, and had healthy beliefs, what would that look like?

An unresolved past can affect you in so many ways. This is something I've learned over and over in the last few years—how old wounds and insecurities don't ever really just "fall off". They shapeshift. They look different in different seasons. But they don't disappear on their own.

Prioritizing your healing is one of the best things you will ever do, and it's this that will break the pattern of self-sabotage more than anything else.

Boundaries

Arguably one of the most important things to understand about yourself is your relationship to boundaries. Placing, setting, holding, and respecting boundaries (both your own and other peoples') are all crucial parts of how you interact with the world.

Boundaries are a very personal thing. How you naturally approach them is often determined in childhood, significantly impacted and affected by how your major relationships treat this area.

A boundary is a line that marks a limit. Typically, personal boundaries represent what you will tolerate and allow, either from yourself or other people. It can be anything from a one-word "no," to the hours you tell your employer you're available to work, an understanding with a romantic partner on how you'll treat each other, or standing up for yourself when someone rips you off.

We all have an idea of what we're willing to accept or offer. Boundaries are simply putting a fence around those things to protect them. They are a *good* and healthy part of any relationship.

The key to understanding both your relationship to boundaries and how to do them well is to answer the question of responsibility.

Whose job is it to make you happy?

Does your employer owe you a fair wage?

Is it okay to tell your friends that they crossed a line?

Can you ask someone to change their behaviour without losing them in your life?

You can't effectively set boundaries without understanding what's on you and what's on others. Without being clear on personal responsibility, someone ends up asking for too much, someone else gets taken advantage of, and ultimately—it all could've been prevented with a few simple boundaries.

Your responsibility

First things first, let's establish what parts of your life *are* your responsibility—what's up to you, what's yours to own, and what you need to manage. This is not an all-inclusive list of every choice you'll ever make (work, school, etc.), but in the context of relationships and boundaries, these are the things that you need to know you own.

1. Your feelings

Understanding that you are responsible for your feelings is one of the most freeing things you can ever do. The reality is that no one else is in charge of making you feel good. Each of us is responsible for our own actions—the words that leave our mouth, the way we interact with other people. But while the people around you bear responsibility for their actions, it's not on them to control how you feel about what they do.

No one else can make you happy. It doesn't matter how much they love you. It's literally not within their control to manage your emotions. Please don't hear this as a dismissal or invalidation in *any way* of what you're feeling. You absolutely have space to process and feel whatever you need to. This does not excuse any unhealthy, selfish, or toxic behaviour. Taking ownership of your feelings doesn't remove anyone's personal responsibility, it only clarifies whose stuff is whose.

When someone hurts you, their actions are *totally* on them. You may want to re-evaluate boundaries, have some hard conversations, and they may have to accept consequences for damaging the relationship. But they can't be responsible for your happiness.

Throughout most of my life, I've had a pretty deep insecurity over not being taken seriously. I look young for my age, and from the time I was a child, I often felt dismissed and left out. It only got worse after publishing that book when I was 10.

Early on when I was in makeup school, after telling a teacher that it bothered me when she laughed at me while I worked, she told me I was "*too cute* to take seriously."

I think she meant it as a compliment, certainly not as an insult. But after spending my senior year of high school sacrificing extracurriculars and social activities to work and try to save enough towards the $20,000 tuition, it wasn't what I was hoping to hear. And in light of this insecurity, it hit a deep, deep nerve.

The thing is, though—my feelings weren't her responsibility. For one, I don't think that she had *any* idea how deep of a wound she was rubbing salt in. Had this not already been a sore point, I probably could've brushed it off and moved on with my day.

Honestly, in that moment, I was pretty upset. But she could not possibly be held responsible for an emotional reaction that largely had nothing to do with her.

Of course, not **all wounds** are unintentional. And it's a lot harder to move on when someone you care about has intentionally hurt you.

The good news about this, though, is that because you are responsible for your feelings, you get to decide what to do with them. While it's absolutely essential to process your feelings, you can also set boundaries for yourself over how much emotional energy you invest in certain relationships. A principle that has rung quite true for me this year is the idea that you shouldn't take criticism from people who you wouldn't take advice from.

Not everyone's opinion of you matters. Taking ownership of your feelings means being responsible for your own healing, but also deciding what voices you want to listen to, what feedback you want to take to heart, and who gets a primary spot in your life.

2. Your relationships

On the same note, your relationships are your responsibility. You get to choose who you want in your life, and to what extent and capacity you'd like them there. One of the best parts about becoming an adult is starting to experience this freedom. As children, we are not in control of who our classmates are, what playdates our parents arrange, or who our co-workers might be in a first job.

But the older you get, the more choices you have. Picking your people is an incredibly important process for so many reasons, and that's something that's entirely up to you.

You have the right to remove someone from your life if you need to. It's important that you know that, especially when it comes to boundaries. Drawing a line with someone does not equate to ending a relationship, but if they refuse to respect what you've asked of them in this relationship, you are absolutely free to walk away. That option is always available to you. Whether or not it's the right call is up to you.

3. Your boundaries

We all have some kind of idea about what our boundaries are. A mental image of which lines are flexible and which are fixed, the expectations we have for the people we're in relationship with, and what would be a dealbreaker for us.

Here's the thing: no one can read your mind.

No friend, significant other, or boss is capable of predicting your expectations or providing you with what you need without being asked.

"If I ask for it, it doesn't count," is an extremely common—and completely unfair— way to treat your partner. Without communicating your needs and boundaries, you cannot expect someone to meet and respect them.

Setting and holding your own boundaries is on you. If there's something you want or really need from someone, you have to ask them for it. It doesn't need to be harsh, and you shouldn't feel the need to apologize for simply being human. When you set boundaries, you're creating your own terms and conditions for what you're willing to allow in your life—and that's *healthy.*

Boundaries will look different relationship to relationship and season to season. They're an ever-changing part of your life. If someone is unwilling to respect the requirements of your friendship—that's their choice. It can feel really, really uncomfortable to be in that situation, but ultimately, you need to know what you're willing to accept and what is non-negotiable for you.

4. Your actions

Finally, your actions are your responsibility. It's absolutely your job to take ownership for your choices. In the same way that you ask others to respect your boundaries, they will ask you to respect theirs. If you want to remain in someone's life, this is a must.

Boundaries are protection for everyone involved. They keep you honest, connected, and true to the relationship you've decided to have. You are within your rights to walk away if someone asks you to maintain a boundary you're not comfortable with, and so are they.

This sounds harsh, but honestly, setting boundaries is usually really productive. It's rare that it ends badly, and if ever it does, it's probably a sign that you're better off to separate.

Not your responsibility

Along with taking ownership of the parts of your life and relationships that are your responsibility, it's really essential to identify what you may be taking on that is *not* your responsibility.

1. Other people's feelings

In the same way that it's no one else's job to maintain your happiness, it's not your job to take care of theirs. That doesn't mean that you shouldn't care about them. Contributing positively to the lives of the people you're close to is kind of important in relationships. But while your actions are yours, you can't control how someone reacts or responds. You can't force something that's not there.

Taking steps to encourage, to uplift, or to try and boost the wellbeing of someone you care about is a healthy thing to do. Taking on the weight of their full emotional state is not.

When your actions hurt someone, apologizing is

probably the best course of action. Take the time to hear someone out, do your best to understand where they're coming from, and honestly look at where you went wrong.

But it's also important to separate what you did from what they felt. Sometimes, the connection is straightforward, but other times, things are more complicated, and you may have to let go of pieces that aren't yours.

2. Other people's choices/actions

You can set all the boundaries you want, form all the ties you'd like, and build relationships strong enough to take on anything. But you can't force someone else to do the same.

Any relationship is a two-way street, and if the people close to you make other choices about how they want to proceed in your relationship, that's on them. If you've communicated your boundaries, asked for what you need, and are committed to doing your part, then let it go.

Boundaries may be seen more in a relational context than an individual one, but they are a direct reflection of how you see yourself.

Your ability to set boundaries is intimately connected to what you think you deserve.

And you are worth being treated well.

Your life is your own, and only you know your story. As you go through life, you will continually discover more and more about who you are and how what you've been through has brought you here.

This process can be painful at first, but cultivating self-awareness can save you from painful regrets and bring you *so much* peace and confidence. With that in mind, as we continue to talk about building the life of your dreams, know that **there is nothing in your past or present that has the ability to define your future or potential except you.**

CHAPTER SEVEN:
Intentional Healing

A couple of years ago, I enrolled in a program designed to help people identify, confront, and heal from the pain and trauma in their life. At the time, I didn't expect all that much to come from it. My world had never been rocked by externally-visible trauma, and I habitually minimized my own feelings and experiences. I figured it would be a good opportunity for growth, however, and I wanted to work through some insecurity that I couldn't seem to shake.

During the program, some old wounds came up for me. They were things that I thought I'd pretty much worked through. I'd let go of the anger, and while I knew there was no justifying what had happened, I'd forgiven the people that hurt me and was ready to move on.

And then one week, the homework was different.

Rather than being asked to write down the details of an event or how I felt in the moment, I was asked the simple question: "What did you come to believe about yourself, others, or the world because of this?"

Oof.

Suddenly, dozens of bits and pieces of my life started to make sense.

Beliefs I'd never questioned, habits that I hadn't been able to break, and unhealthy behaviours I could never understand became visible in a whole new way.

Trauma doesn't end because a situation does. Wounds don't disappear just because you pretend they're not there. Our life experiences, particularly the painful ones, have a way of sinking into our unconscious minds without us even noticing.

The major events of our lives are not ones we forget. But they often affect us in more ways than we are even aware of. Fear, anxiety, insecurity, and self-doubt can all be long-term ripples from one serious impact.

These things affect you, whether you know it or not. Our brains are sponges—

and the things we absorb have the potential to wind up deep in our psyche. You are constantly communicating the messages you believe to yourself and others, setting expectations and ideas about the future.

This is, of course, most visible in childhood, when

your ideas of right, wrong, good, bad, and normal are all determined by what you are exposed to and taught. Even beliefs you were never explicitly told about can become strong, lifelong ones, simply because you observed a reaction.

This is partly just how your brain functions, and there's no shame in that. But for this reason, it's important to practice intentionality in your actions, because if you're not mindful of your thoughts and motives, you can end up following an unconscious set of ideals that doesn't line up with your actual priorities.

Cultivating self-awareness in all areas of life is incredibly important, but perhaps none so much as your own healing. You're still human, and life is still life. When you go through hard things, they will affect you in some way or another. And the major events of our lives are rarely, if ever, neutral. At the end of the day, intentionality doesn't stop you from getting burned from time to time.

For better or worse, suffering and hardship are often the things that make us who we are. They can teach us strength or weakness, pain or love, how to forgive or how to hate. Things aren't always that black and white, but we do walk away from trauma with *something*, whether we like it or not.

The good news: you can be an active participant in deciding what that is.

You get to decide how to define this situation, what

it means to heal, and what you want to believe walking out of it. Being rejected by someone doesn't have to make you a rejected person. Getting fired doesn't mean you're incompetent. But if we're not aware of what we're thinking, these ideas may take root without us even noticing it.

We don't get to control what happens to us, but we do get to decide a piece of what we do with it.

Healing is often talked about as if it's simply moving on. Forgetting about it, distracting yourself, replacing what was lost. But that's not healing.

Whether it's a sharp insult, a broken heart or physical trauma—when something cuts deep, it stays deep. Buried inside of us, these wounds have a way of coming out throughout our lives.

Personal growth—or "intentional healing"—is diving into this. Addressing your deepest pain points, confronting the things that you're afraid of, and choosing to set yourself free. It's not a glamorous process, but it is a *necessary* one.

As author Brianna Wiest writes, "Self-care is often a very unbeautiful thing."[1]

The image often pitched to us of caring for our mental health is very different, though. It's bubble baths and candles, wine and paint nights, cute home decor, and trendy affirmations. Those aren't *bad* things. But it doesn't matter how great it smells, your Mahogany Teakwood candle can't confront limiting beliefs, help you overcome trauma, or teach you to set boundaries.

Relaxing is great, and it's an important part of a balanced life. But it can also be a distraction. A way of avoiding pain.

Making yourself feel good so that you don't have to address the things that make you feel bad.

The thing about purposeful growth is that without it, you may as well throw away the idea of intentional living right now. Without working through the things that lurk within your mind and heart, without acknowledging and understanding how your past affects your present and future, you will have a near-impossible time trying to connect with what you really want out of life.

Whether you're a follower of Jesus or not, you've likely heard the saying "Love your neighbour as yourself." It's often repeated and rarely explained, but several months ago, I was talking to someone who had a unique take on the subject—

As they pointed out, loving yourself is inevitable. Even when you feel like you hate yourself, you love yourself. The opposite of love is not hate, it's indifference. "Self-love" in its most basic form isn't something we can escape. It's wired into us. Like it or not, you matter to you. If you didn't love yourself, at least in some capacity, you wouldn't care to feel anything about yourself.

We are almost always going to instinctively act in our own best interest. Because of this, the way we perceive ourselves and our identities really, really matters. The key to doing life well is to understand what "*good*" really means to you. When you walk through life carrying undealt-with baggage, it's really hard to get a clear view of what that is, and even harder to cultivate it.

Fear, self-sabotage, and uncontrolled emotions end up calling a lot of the shots—and they don't usually lead to the best results.

Trauma-based mindsets

In my experience, trauma has often looked like internal bleeding. Graphic, I know, but stick with me for a minute on this—say you get injured somehow. A car accident, a bad fall. You emerge with some visible wounds. Cuts, scrapes, bruises. They're painful, and anyone can tell just by looking at them.

Even if you wanted to, you can't ignore these injuries. They are literally staring you in the face. So you do what you need to do to heal them. See a doctor, take your medicine. It takes a while, but over time the injuries either fade into scars or disappear entirely.

What you didn't see right away, though, was what went on *inside* of your body. Adrenaline, excitement, and the obvious wounds that demanded your attention took priority. In theory, of course, you'd hope that the medical team caring for you would catch it—but sometimes our real-life support systems are not as observant or adept at catching these things as we'd like them to be.

Over time, the adrenaline goes down, and your body starts to turn its attention to the internal injuries. They're bad. They may have started small, and their effects weren't as immediately obvious, but by the time you notice them, they've been bleeding for quite some time.

This is often how emotional wounds play out. When you go through something—a breakup, the loss of someone you love, a harsh rejection—it's natural to focus on the obvious wounds. The symptoms and external cues as to what's really going on.

After a breakup, you'll probably feel pretty sad. The end of a relationship can be devastating. More often than not, you and the people you love will focus on restoring your happiness rather than healing.

You might work on cheering yourself up. Doing fun things, putting a smile back on your face. You'll try not to think about it. Distract yourself with whatever works and address the wounds you can *see.*

But then what happens? When those ultra-visible wounds heal? When you remember how to have a good time and put a smile on your face? Will you recognize it when the bleeding starts to come out? When it begins to affect your future relationships and your self-esteem?

Most people don't. I didn't, for a long time.

Trauma changes you. Pain changes you. There isn't a way for it *not* to. But even though you can't decide to be unaffected, to stay the same, you *can* decide to let it make you better. To learn and heal and grow instead of letting your scars call the shots and run your life.

This is a short chapter.

That's intentional (ha), but it's not because this principle is less important than any others. Your journey of healing has a massive effect on your day-to-day quality of life and on what the future will look like for you.

But it's also a very intimate, deeply personal process—one perhaps better explored in a manner more specific to you.

If you have the option to pursue therapy or counselling, do it. Whether you feel like you need it or not, having someone to talk to makes a world of difference. In addition, see the resources page at the back of this book for more information, suggestions, and resources to connect you with tools to support you in whatever you're working through.

CHAPTER EIGHT:
Community

n 1938, Harvard researchers launched what is known as the Harvard Study of Adult Development.[1] Beginning during the Great Depression, the study has followed the lives of 724 different men—tracking their careers, health, happiness, circumstances, and relationships. The study was split into two groups— the first, participants who were current students at Harvard College (including future U.S. president John F. Kennedy), and the second, a group of young boys from Boston's poorest neighbourhoods.

The study has been running ever since, eventually beginning to track the men's spouses and children as well. And the findings are *fascinating*. According to the current and fourth director of the study, Robert Waldinger, there are tens of thousands of pages of information collected throughout this study—and with all of it, he said this:

"The lessons aren't about wealth or fame or working harder and harder. The clearest message that we get from this 75-year study is this: good relationships keep us happier and healthier. Period."[2]

This is one of the world's longest-running studies of adult life ever. Its goal was to reveal information about what kept people happy and well, and it did just that. But the answer wasn't juice cleanses or social status or career accomplishment.

It was *community* that made the biggest difference.

Isn't that fascinating? Regardless of socioeconomic status, promotions, income, and family life—quality relationships proved to be the defining factor in someone's life.

Human connection is essential. It's a foundational part of what it means to be alive. We need each other, and on some level, we know it.

There's this idea going around in the self-help community—that the reason that you should love yourself is because you don't want to ever rely on someone else. That the reason you should be strong is so you don't have to ask for help.

It's this subtle suggestion that you ought to be able, on your own, to accomplish anything and everything you set your mind to. You should never need or expect support or community, and if you don't do something on your own, it doesn't really count.

Well—here's the thing. That's super weird. Also, very unhealthy. And not really true.

There are things that you *can't* do on your own. We're all limited by our physical ability, emotional capacity, hours in a day, etc., and for the record, limitations aren't a bad thing. Understanding your own boundaries is actually quite freeing. It allows you to prioritize more effectively and to understand how to best use your time.

What you are capable of will change throughout your life, as different seasons hold different realities. Building a healthy relationship with your own limits and getting comfortable asking for help will serve you well in all areas of life. There's no need to be ashamed of your own humanity.

To be honest with you, even if you *can* do something entirely by yourself, there are many times where it's not wise to. In writing this book, I consulted different editors, friends, and family members, as well as the work of many authors, writers, psychologists, research papers, and articles, because, while in theory, I could've slapped some words on paper by myself, these perspectives and input added *so much.*

Asking for help is by far the quickest way to increase your potential. On your own, your limitations are fixed. Whatever you can do is what you can do. That's fine, but when you collaborate in community with other people, your limits are widened exponentially.

Whether it's writing a book, raising a child, a work project, or relationship, opening yourself up to support and connection can increase the quality of *everything around you*—even just your everyday life.

We weren't meant to do life alone. It's not how we're wired.

And according to the aforementioned Harvard study, healthy, lifegiving community is *the* defining factor in your overall happiness.

Of course, that refers to more than simply being in the presence of other people. It's not enough to just be in a crowd or make small talk at the water cooler. Real community is not a flimsy, meaningless, schoolgirl crush.

It's not putting your value in other people or seeking validation from external sources. Those aren't the kind of relationships that make you whole or happy.

Real community is *healthy relationships* with people who are committed to showing up for you. People who celebrate you when you win, and grieve with you when you lose. Friends that are just as present when life gets messy as they are when you're on top of the world.

It's two-sided relationships with individuals who are building on a foundation of mutual love, trust, and respect. These kinds of real, raw, friendships aren't "easy." They require effort and sacrifice in the same way that a romantic relationship does, but they are also one of the *most valuable* things you could ever have.

In the same way that intentional living doesn't keep you from the realities of what it means to be human in the world, intentional community doesn't shield you from pain. But it does mean that you don't have to shoulder it alone. You're part of something bigger. A team, a family—whatever you want to call it. Community is my favourite word, because I think it applies *so* well to what relationships should look like in your life.

A group of people *can* be a community, but sometimes they're just a group. A neighborhood *can* be a community, but sometimes it's just houses.

A *community* is an environment of fellowship—doing life together, choosing to share each other's burdens, joys, experiences, and everything else. It's not something you fall into, but something that you choose to commit to and be a part of—something that makes you better.

Sounds pretty great, doesn't it? But getting there can feel like an impossible task.

I know I grew up craving relationships like this, and I really believed that actually having them was the exception, not the rule. I spent the better part of my life hungry, desiring to be a part of a community, with no clue how to make that a reality.

Upon reflection, my biggest challenge wasn't that I

hadn't found the right people, but that I didn't know what it meant to be an active part of a community. If all you know how to do is be on your own, simply getting dropped into a group of people does nothing.

Authentic community takes time, roots, and relationships. It requires patience and demands vulnerability. But building it from scratch sounds harder than it is.

In all likelihood, most of the people around you are just as eager for this kind of community as you are. Many have claimed we are living in a "loneliness epidemic," and to some extent, this is undoubtedly true. Blame it on whatever you want—

social media, cancel culture, politics, or any combination—we're here now, and we're stuck. We're isolated. And we really, really need each other.

It's not up to you to save the world or fix other people's loneliness, but it's probably not as hard as you think to resolve your own. Finding your people can be a lifelong journey, but that doesn't equate to a lifetime of searching. You can build community wherever you're at, make connections anywhere you go, and accelerate your growth by investing in quality relationships.

The Chameleon Effect

It's a common adage that you are the sum total of the people you spend the most time with. While it's not entirely true, it's not untrue either. Human beings have a deep desire to be seen, accepted, and chosen, and one of the ways we try to fulfill this is by fitting in with the people around us. It's not always, or even *often* a conscious choice to be influenced—we simply imitate what we experience.

Have you ever picked up a local accent while travelling, or accidentally mimicked the slang terms of a friend from a different area or dialect? You're not alone.

In a 1999 study, researchers from NYU gathered information on what they called "The Chameleon Effect."[3] One of their experiments was to take a study participant and team them up with a hired actor—who was introduced to the participant as a fellow member of the study. They were given simple tasks, and as they completed them, the actors would begin exhibiting certain small mannerisms—rubbing their face, tapping their feet, etc.

The participants quickly followed suit, seemingly entirely without their knowledge. They picked up the habits of the actors without even meaning to. Afterwards, they completed a reverse of the study. Rather than the actors initiating behaviours, they were instructed to mimic any habits of the participants around them.

Ultimately, the participants responded very well to this. The actors mimicking their behaviour came across more likeable, particularly when compared with actors who simply remained neutral.

Copying others is more than just a grade school annoyance or a younger sibling habit. It's built into us. We observe, learn, and are heavily influenced by others, even when we don't notice it. The effect is only made stronger when it's someone whose opinion and approval we value highly.

Who you spend time with matters. Like it or not, you are affecting each other in thought and in action. It's for this reason that finding *your* people, rather than just *some* people, is important.

It's not *that* hard to find people who can tolerate you. But your people aren't just bodies in a room— they are the extension of a chosen family. Your people are the collective that you click with. They're the ones you decide to do life with, to walk with and stand beside both when things are hard and when they are wonderful.

They're the ones you choose and who choose you back. These relationships are life-giving, encouraging, and offer genuine value to your life. Your people are committed to you, and you are committed to them. But before you can find them, you need to figure out exactly what you want in the people who hold such an influential spot in your life.

How to find your people

When I was in 8th grade, one of my teachers was very passionate about what she considered "community building." She frequently had us set aside our books to discuss the ways in which we as a class had failed to build community well. I remember listening to her scold us for having friend groups, arguing that there was absolutely no reason that small sectors of our class should hang out exclusively—that we shouldn't spend time with some people and not others.

Even at 13, that made no sense to me. High schoolers—and, let's be honest, adults—can be ridiculously cliquey. Exclusive, cold to outsiders, unwelcoming, and none of that is acceptable. Especially as adults. We can and need to do better than that.

But at the same time, you can't be best friends with everyone—and trying to do so usually doesn't lead to emotional health or safety.

Selective kindness is incompatible with limitless grace. As a Christian, as someone who has received and benefitted from the undeserved and overwhelming grace of God, there is absolutely no explanation, excuse, or acceptable reason to turn around and deprive someone of basic kindness because they "don't deserve it." I don't deserve what I've been given, and to withhold the simplest common grace from someone else is unbiblical and extraordinarily wrong.

But selective *intimacy*, on the other hand, is wisdom.

Not everyone should have access to the deepest parts of you. Not everyone should have equal impact, standing, or priority in your life.

It's often easier to prioritize categories of your life—hobbies, side projects, dreams—than it is to rank the people around you. But on some level, you have to know that you cannot be a friend to everyone and do it well. At some point, you need to select which relationships are ones you want to fully invest in. To put your heart, soul, and time into and commit to showing up for.

About a year ago, I did a very honest assessment of the people in my life—the relationships that I had. I felt like I wasn't showing up enough for the ones that mattered the most to me, and in order to change that, I had to take some steps back in other ones.

Now, I didn't cut anyone off or actually end any of the friendships that I had—but in order to dedicate the time I needed to the people who meant the most to me, I took my foot off of the gas in some of those relationships. I still care about, love, and am in touch with all of those people—but they're not key parts of my community, and I am not a key part of theirs. And that's okay.

Being picky with your people isn't a bad thing—in fact, it's necessary in order to maintain healthy relationships. There are so many wonderful, valuable, incredible individuals in the world *who are not for you.*

You can care deeply about someone and at the same time know that you're not meant to be one of the most important parts of their lives.

All that to say—knowing who your people are has as much to do with what you don't want in someone as what you do. There's a level on which it's similar to picking a romantic partner. Everyone's needs and wants are different in relationships, even platonic ones.

Think about the things that you really want in your people. What kind of community would you be eager and excited to be a part of and contribute to? What kind of space would push you to grow, help you become better, and support your long term goals for the kind of life you want?

There are few non-negotiables when it comes to friends, because there is no one-size-fits all. That said, as you reflect on the relationships that you have and consider what you might want them to look like down the line, make sure that these three key characteristics are present.

1. Respect

Healthy friendships require respect. There has to be some kind of mutual understanding that you are both equals and can honor the other's existence, value, and boundaries. In all likelihood, some of the people closest to you will share your beliefs and values—but not all of them. Sometimes you may disagree about what's most important, your world-views, how to respond to a given situation.

Disagreement isn't a problem. In fact, it's really healthy, and having good relationships with people that are different from you is a huge sign of growth. Challenging your own thoughts and ideas is the only way to be sure of them, and it's also the only way to consider when you might be wrong. Having safe spaces for those important conversations is a huge gift.

For the most important relationships in your life, you should be able to talk, connect, and share even if you disagree. Those differences can make the relationship richer, not thinner. It's not always easy, but with respect at the center of a close relationship, that should never be an issue.

Conflict, complications, and working through basic issues is inevitable when you're spending a lot of time with someone, but general respect should never be something that's up for debate. Ultimately, you need to be able to trust each other's intentions, hearts, and be okay agreeing to disagree.

2. Some sense of shared values

While quality friendships don't require you to be on the same page all the time, or even most of the time, there should be some sense of shared values. It's one thing to have different values than your casual friends, acquaintances, and co-workers.

But when it comes to the people who speak into your life, the ones you go to for advice, and lean on for support—being on similar pages is kind of important.

In all honesty, it's this connection that often bonds a community together. You may be in different life stages, career paths, or locations, but the overarching goals and priorities you have for life should line up at least in part.

Together, you are pursuing a particular kind of life. Not all friendships have that in common, nor do they need to, but being immersed in a group where you can be encouraged and challenged in that way will *transform* your personal growth and development.

Note: If the only people who speak into your life and opinions are people who think exactly like you do, you will likely end up with a very narrow and limited view of the world. It's really worth pursuing relationships with people who've lived different experiences. Getting to hear other stories, perspectives, and backgrounds, both in the everyday and on big issues is really important.

3. Commitment & Consistency

A community is made up of people who are committed to being in your life. That doesn't mean that they don't have other things going in, or that they'll always be available at the drop of a hat, but merely that they're not planning on walking out or disappearing on you. They're reliable and consistent.

These things aren't always obvious at first, but over time, you'll get a pretty good idea of who's in it for the long haul. Your people will be present for you. Their loyalty won't flip based on opportunity, and you'll know that you can lean on them when you need to.

You don't have to make a blood pact to be in each others' lives forever, but the intent to build long-term relationships results in more meaningful connections.

People are delightfully imperfect. We are ever-changing, growing, learning and becoming different and new. This is just part of life, and as you learn to be picky with your friends and choose who you're close to, remember that you're all going through this process together.

As you change, hold space for the people around you to do the same. Stay committed to growing together, and look for opportunities to take on new adventures and challenges as a collective.

How to build intentional community

Finding your people is one of the most important things you'll ever do. Building a community of friendships, especially when they have the potential to last, will grow you and build into you in ways only comparable to romantic relationships. Closeness to other people is challenging—you inevitably deal with conflict, differences, scheduling, and a whole host of other stuff—but man, oh man, is it worth it.

There's this 2005 chick flick—The Sisterhood of the Traveling Pants—that I *loved* growing up. Blake Lively, America Ferrera, Alexis Bledel and Amber Tamblyn were my dream friend group. It was that ideal, easy, comfortable space, where you might not always get along, but you all love each other so much that it doesn't matter. I've yet to find magic jeans, but I have found friendships like that. More often than not, though, they don't happen accidentally.

If you are one of the lucky few who was born and raised into a strong community, where you simply came out of the womb surrounded by best friends—I'm so happy for you. That wasn't the case for me, and it's not for most of us. As a kid, teenager, or university student, school is likely the primary source of human contact, but entering the adult world, it can be a lot harder to meet people.

Initiation

The best and most effective way to find your people is to simply start being an initiator. Rather than waiting for things to fall into place, get invited out, or to have a reason to hit the town, create your own opportunities.

Start conversations on your own. Instead of waiting for someone to reach out to you, reach out to them. One of the best ways to start doing this is to give people compliments. Everyone loves hearing nice things about themselves, and it's so, so easy to make them feel good.

Most of the time people simply smile, say thank you, and move on with their day. But when you get in the habit of this, you'll notice that sometimes, they stick around for a minute. They may want to chat, compliment you back, or just be happy to connect. Depending on the setting, this can be a great conversation starter.

When I first moved to Vancouver, I was 17, fresh out of high school and desperate for community. After a few months of floundering, I accidentally discovered this method when I started taking regular walks around my neighbourhood.

I developed a habit of telling everyone I came across who was walking a dog that their dogs were cute. It wasn't meant to be anything big. I'm just a dog person and I like being able to make people's day (literally everyone wants to hear that their dog is cute).

To my surprise, this simple comment started so many sweet interactions and opened up a lot of doors in terms of getting to know people. Since then, I've started using it more often and in other ways. If you're not naturally outgoing, something like this can be a great way to practice initiation where there's no real consequences if it goes badly.

The bolder you can be, the easier it is. Invite someone to hang out. Ask a coworker to grab coffee. See if that person you always run into at the gym wants to go for lunch. Make the first move.

Can it feel weird at first? Yeah.

But at the end of the day, if you want to find your people, being an initiator is the fastest way to do it.

I probably would not have become close with my best friend, started dating my boyfriend, or even *met* most of the important people in my life without this method. Relationships matter, and we all know it **—but waiting for other people to come to us is like giving up before we've even started.**

When you catch yourself feeling down or lonely because no one's invited you to hang out recently, ask yourself when you last tried to initiate plans. Relationships are a two-way street, and it's your responsibility to cultivate the community in your own life.

Authenticity

While picking and finding your people is a process done over time, the best way you can start building community *right now* is to focus on **becoming the kind of person that you would want to be close to.**

An intentional community is a space where everyone who enters feels safe. Where they feel welcomed, valued, and wanted. People don't just want to be met, they want to be seen and known. In order to create this kind of an environment, you need to be willing to set the tone.

Those characteristics that you want to look for in friends—respect, values, commitment—do you exhibit them too? Any successful relationship has effort and dedication from both sides, and learning to do this well is a necessary step in deepening your relationships.

As you think about the things that you desire from others, whether that's trust, encouragement, showing up for each other, or anything else, look for opportunities to practice offering that to other people. Whatever expectations you have for your closest friends, you need to have equal or higher standards for yourself.

**Authenticity is the baseline
for a successful community.**

Being real about who you are, what you're going

through, and what matters *has to happen* if you're to create any real relationships.

Opening yourself up to other people is intimidating. It creates the potential for rejection, and that can be scary. But without that first step, it is literally impossible to get close to someone. Bold authenticity doesn't always feel natural or safe, and sometimes it's not.

Not everyone you meet will end up as a part of your community—some you just won't click with (and may not want to be friends with). Some will have lives that are already full. And others, honestly, may not want to be friends with you.

But just because you're not for *everyone* doesn't mean that there's no one for you.

Selective intimacy is a *good thing*. And it's worth getting through a few rejections to find a group of people that you actually want to do life with. But the only way you're going to know if you really click with someone is if you take that step to show up and be yourself.

Vulnerability

Taking emotional risks is a necessary part of this. Building intentional community requires you to get out of your comfort zone, be more honest than you normally would be, and share the parts of you that you may be tempted to hide.

Typically speaking, you get out of a relationship what you put into it. You can only go as deep with people as you are willing to let them see. When you're vulnerable with others, you open the door for strong, long-lasting relationships. This creates a chance to bond in a different way, to be seen fully, and to be affirmed in spite of the darkest and deepest parts of you.

Vulnerability is admitting your mistakes. It's owning up to reality. Asking for help when you need it.

In her *incredible* book on the subject, author Brene Brown writes this: "Vulnerability sounds like truth and feels like courage. Truth and courage aren't always comfortable, but they're never weakness."[4]

Being vulnerable with other people is one of the bravest and boldest things you can do. Showing up and being real with your community carries impact. The more vulnerable you are, the safer others will feel being vulnerable *with you*.

Nothing builds trust quite like this.

Showing up

Consistency in community goes a long way. People will change, life will change, but one thing that should never change in a valued relationship is the fact that you show up for each other.

Intentional friendships and communities are made up of people whose commitment supersedes convenience. Living life alongside someone means being there for the wins and the losses. Having their back when they need you.

Showing up for people isn't about grand gestures or saying the right thing, it's simply choosing to be present in the little moments as well as the big ones. Sometimes it's dropping off groceries, sending an encouraging text, or just sitting in silence when there's no words left to express.

It's the simplest of principles, and yet it's often overlooked. Showing up requires planning ahead and it's almost impossible to be consistent without prioritizing certain relationships in your life. You can't show up for everyone.

This doesn't mean that you have to drop everything because your friend had a rough day. You still have other commitments and areas of life. But finding a way to let them know that they matter and you're thinking about them is easier than you might think.

Celebration

Celebration is one of the best ways to build deep relationships quickly. I can tell you without a doubt that the people I feel the closest to are the ones that I know are on my team, the people who will have my back no matter what, and who celebrate me big when I win. They're the ones who show up on my birthday instead of sending a text, who tell me that they're proud of me for any bit of progress, and who make sure that I know that I am loved.

It's sometimes easier to show up for people in the hard times than in the good. Watching someone you care about struggle usually makes you want to help them. But what about when they're finding success—and you're not?

What then?

If competition is present in your relationship, celebration will be hard. It's because of this that the friends who *do* celebrate you often end up being your closest.

Like so many parts of a community-minded relationship, the art of celebration isn't defined by one moment in your relationship. It's a pattern, and over time, consistently showing up to cheer on your friends will do more for your relationship than one pity party or shared hard moment ever could.

Relationships are made up of habits just like any other area of life—and the patterns you display are constantly communicating with the people around you. The way that you show up for your community says more about your feelings and commitment than your words ever could.

Finding your people matters.

Picking the right people matters.

But *none of it* is that significant unless you too are

preparing for the kind of community that you crave. To some extent, you'll attract what you put out, and if you're looking for quality friends, you start by being one.

More than just bodies in a room or a way to kill time, the people that we're surrounded with are connected to our very identity. They are shaping us, affecting us, and building into our lives.

The findings from the Harvard Study of Adult Development showed that relationships were more than just having people around you. Even unhappy people have others in their lives. Relationship quality had a *huge* role to play in the participants' wellbeing, just as it does in yours.

We need each other. And we need to learn to love each other well. Be *bold* in your pursuit of meaningful relationships, authentic with the people that you care about, and consistent in creating a life around community. Your happiness may just depend on it.

CHAPTER NINE:
A Love on Purpose

"I**t's either him or someone better."**
I have no idea how many times I've said those words. To friends, coworkers, family. Some people I knew well and some I didn't.

I shared them boldly—feeling confident in my attempts to encourage the people I knew to be struggling in relationships with words of wisdom. My thinking was this: to my friends who were either going through a breakup or terrified to let go, be bold, say or do the hard things—remember that it's either him or someone better.

Well-intentioned, yes, but severely misguided. I didn't even see the flaw in my thinking until I found myself in the same situation, and began receiving the same sympathetic messages.

"There's other fish in the sea..."

"When you meet the one God has for you..."

"If it's not him, it's someone better..."

I couldn't figure out why it bothered me as much as it did. I knew it was said in love, and while I appreciated the sentiment and time that people took to encourage me, I was okay being single. I wasn't hurting because I was alone. I was hurting because I had to say goodbye to someone whom I loved deeply.

So the whole "There's other fish in the sea" statement felt almost condescending and discrediting of the grieving stage I was in.

Never in my life had I felt so instantly safe and trusting with someone. A complete lack of insecurity in a relationship for the first time created a ground for fast-developing feelings and vulnerability in new ways. I was known, loved, and cared for in a way that I hadn't been before.

I shared things that I'd never shared without fear. Laughed harder than I can remember laughing in years. Parts of myself that I'd forgotten about showed themselves, and I felt freedom.

It was a connection affirmed not only by both of us, but many around us who watched us interact. Bold predictions were made about where things were going and how they would end up, and I let myself dream.

And then it was over.

And the safety,

And the laughter,

The car rides,

The movie nights,

The milkshakes,

And the comfort

Was

Just

Gone.

So the text messages and phone calls, telling me that "if it's not him, it's someone better" only stung.

Because here's the thing—relationships are not a guarantee in life. You will not find a single scripture, affirmation, or motivational speaker who can promise you a life partner. That certainty doesn't exist.

Love is a deeply important part of the world we live in—but being loved by a romantic partner (or not) has *no* effect on your worth as a human being. It's not a badge of honour. **There is no human relationship that can alter your value.**

Culturally, however, we are often pitched a different message. The idea that your soulmate, your "One," your person is out there and waiting for you is constantly being pushed on us. We are led to chase romance, expect fairytales, and trust that one day, we will find our other half.

But what if we don't?

In a book about purposeful action, it would be wrong not to touch on the significant impact that romantic relationships have on our lives—and what it means to do those intentionally—but I cannot write this chapter without first clarifying that *you are enough on your own.* A partner cannot make you whole, happy, or complete.

Wanting a relationship isn't a bad thing. Making it a part of your core identity, however, can be extremely dangerous.

Don't get me wrong—I'm a total romantic. I believe in love and butterflies and marriage and staying together forever. I have had the immense privilege of knowing great love, and from it, I have learned more about what it means to be intentional than almost anything else.

In my experience, there's nothing quite like falling in love to show you just how broken some parts of you are. Relationships have a way of revealing your greatest fears, insecurities, and wounds like nothing else. The vulnerability of a relationship tends to expose the parts of us that we've hidden even from ourselves—and that can be heavy.

But love is also the greatest gift I've ever known.

Love might reveal the worst parts of you, but it also allows you to see the best. A healthy relationship is one where you are not only safe, but encouraged to be yourself. Watching someone else know you, choose you, and love you can remind you of all the reasons why they should.

Love comes in more forms than one, and romantic love isn't the be-all, end-all of life—but it is an important one. The people we are close to have a *huge* impact on who we are and who we become. The emotions of falling in love, or out of it, are some of the most powerful ones we can experience.

They can burn us, break us, or shape us into an entirely different person. Whether a relationship is forever or not, if it's real, it'll change you. So whatever your ultimate relationship goals are, knowing how to *love well* is one of the most important skills you'll ever develop.

The worst thing about the breakup that I went through wasn't the condescending comments. It wasn't that I was single. It wasn't the adjustment to a different way of life.

It was that *our connection and our feelings were never an issue.* The love was real. The feelings were real. The compatibility was there. But things got complicated, and we had *no clue* how to handle it well. Intentionality in relationships was not an idea I was familiar with at the time, and even if I'd heard the concept, I would have had no idea how to actually implement it.

Like intentional living itself, purposeful love has no official definition—but it more or less comes down to this—what kind of love do you want?

In the same way that living your life on purpose requires your active participation, a relationship you are truly committed to needs your effort, action, and dedication.

Intentionality in relationships is as simple as investing targeted or purposeful effort.

Perhaps the most dangerous idea about love pitched to us through the media is that it just happens. The initial feelings, of course, can happen this way—you fall hard and fast, infatuation takes over, and before you know it, you're madly in love.

But ask a couple that's been together for a few decades what keeps their relationship strong, and you will *never* hear the answer "Oh, it just happens."

Love is an emotion, but it's also a verb—maintaining a long-term relationship requires action. Great love may find you by itself, but it won't stick around forever if you don't take care of it. To love is to be human, but to love and love *well* demands consistent intentionality.

It's not just showing up with flowers, holding a boombox over your head, or getting the right ring.

It's loving the people around you in the way that they feel loved. Staying consistent to your word. Showing up in the good times and the bad.

While this chapter centers on romantic relationships, these principles are *every bit as valid and relevant* in friendships, work relationships, and any close bond with someone you care about.

Relationship Myths

Aphrodite and Adonis. Mr. Darcy and Elizabeth Bennet. Romeo and Juliet. Since the beginning of time, we've been talking about love.

From Ancient Mythology to Hallmark Christmas movies, human affection and connection sucks us in like nothing else. Passion, intensity, and tragedy grab hold of us. And as we hear about love, we fall for the idea itself.

Throughout our lives, and particularly the early years, our idea of love and relationships is being formed. Whatever we see often becomes our idea of "normal."

While this has produced some of the greatest literary works of all time, it's also created a lot of warped ideas of what love is.

A bad breakup can leave you scarred, but an unconscious belief about what a healthy relationship is can do just as much damage—if not more.

There are so many straight-up lies about what love really is that it can be hard to know where to start. It's especially challenging if you didn't grow up watching a strong, healthy relationship, which, statistically speaking, most people don't.

These relationship myths can be incredibly toxic and highly problematic. Not only do they create a false idea of what love should look like (Allie and Noah are not actually couple goals), but they don't give you the tools to even approach relationships from a healthy standpoint.

Whether you're in a relationship right now, you someday hope to be, or you just want to learn to love your friends better, confronting these commonly-held misbeliefs about love will challenge you in the best way.

The fix-it myth

It's a tale as old as time. Good girl meets bad boy (or vice versa, but it seems to go this way in Hollywood). He's damaged, mysterious, and treats everyone else like garbage. But not her. She knows she can fix him. After the dramatic and totally predictable problem arises, they fix everything with their love and ride off into the sunset on his motorcycle.

Except that's not usually how it goes. Entering into a relationship with the desire to "fix" or change a part of the person you're with is always, always a bad idea.

People might change, but they don't do it just because you want them to. Certain habits or behaviours might be negotiable, but their actual person is not something that's going to flip overnight, and if it seems like it does, it *can't* be genuine.

Asking someone to change for you often ends up being manipulative, whether or not that's the intention. Love only works when it's freely given. To make your affection conditional on someone altering part of themselves is not fair, kind, or healthy.

If you can't accept them as they are, there is a strong possibility that the version of them you are in love with doesn't truly exist.

Eventually, these kinds of relationships usually wind up filled with resentment. It's not fair to either of you. Also, as a word of caution—if your significant other treats others poorly, you're probably not the exception—they're just on their best behaviour. When comfort sets in and the gloves come off, that's the treatment you can expect.

I say this because I have been there—I get how badly you can want to be the person that they'll change for. But if they were really ready to be better and to give you what they keep telling you you deserve, they would have done it by now.

No one is perfect. Everyone will have flaws, and pushing your significant other to grow in healthy ways isn't a bad thing. But making your love and future dependent on a version of them that doesn't currently exist is a breeding ground for heartbreak.

The "red flag" myth

A few years ago, I heard a talk on relationships from a pastor who forever changed the way I saw dating. He told this story about when he and his wife of many decades had first met and begun dating. Now in a thriving relationship, he explicitly pointed out the red flags that they'd each displayed in their early relationship.

They both carried baggage. And, he argued, so do you.

The thing about red flags is that *literally everyone* has some. There is not a person on this earth without some baggage, brokenness, and history that they bring into a relationship. Whether it's trauma from an ex, a complicated family history, or low self-esteem, the things you each struggle with will always affect your partner in some way.

Someone *having* red flags is inevitable. But instead of simply looking for an out or creating unrealistic expectations for a match, the important thing is knowing how to deal with them.

In a romantic relationship, you're exposed to someone in a way that no one else is. You see sides of them that friends and family members don't get to.

There is a powerful opportunity to both witness and work through whatever challenges they bring into a relationships.

Seeing brokenness in another person shouldn't be surprising. The question is not "Do they have flaws?" but "What do they do with them?"

If your long-term goal is to find a life partner, it's **much** more important to observe the way that they handle their issues than to count them at the start. When something comes up that concerns you, bring it up. Don't keep it to yourself or maintain stress and resentment without at least having a conversation.

How do they handle being called out? Are they defensive, uncomfortable, open?

These discussions are crucial to maintaining a healthy relationship. No one is perfect, but finding someone who can acknowledge and consciously grow from their bad habits is more reliable than finding someone who seems to get it all right the first time.

In the early stages of a relationship, you often see the things you share with someone more than anything else. You focus on the butterflies, look at the ways they just **get** you and appreciate the little things that they do to make your day.

But they're not always going to get that stuff right. Their innate humanness means that at some point, they're going to screw up—then what?

Having room to grow doesn't necessarily mean a relationship has to end, but it does mean you need to start paying attention. What do they do when they screw up? Are they eager to do better? If you asked them to handle something differently, would they?

Integrity is worth more than instincts. Consistency in character goes a *lot* farther than charm.

If you are approaching relationships with the goal of finding a life partner, it is well worth seeking one out who values growth and can handle criticism.

Please note: There are, of course, red flags that ARE and SHOULD be deal breakers. Abuse of any kind is not something to wait out. Respect is a non-negotiable. Safety is a must. You have *every right* to see a red flag and run. If you know something's not right, even if you can't put your finger on why, know that you are free to leave. Working through challenges is only worth it if you want to be with someone—and if the relationship is a toxic or dangerous one, walk away.

The soulmate myth

It's such a nice idea. It really is—that there is one person out there who was born to complete you. That God, the universe, or some higher power is working to bring you together against all odds.

There's this idea of love that proposes your soulmate

is a mind-reading, yin to your yang, perfect match for you. That they will compliment you perfectly. You'll know them when you see them, you'll understand each other instantly, and it will be easy and fun and wonderful 24/7. It's a thrill, a rush, to imagine that kind of love. But unfortunately, that's not really how it works—and that's GOOD news.

In theory, a soulmate sounds great. Particularly if you're exhausted with the modern dating scene, the thought that your other half is out there somewhere, working their way to you, is a really special one. But to be honest, that's just not how it works.

You might really click with someone, or feel strongly connected, but they will never be able to read your mind. There is no "perfect" match for you.

And that's a good thing! From a numbers perspective, there are a lot of people that any one of us could end up with—and probably several potential options we could be really happy with. Life would look different with each, of course, but it would still go on, and possibly quite well.

It is an incredibly freeing thing to embrace the understanding that *you get to choose.* You have the freedom to decide what matters most to you in life and who you want as your partner in it. Your values, goals, and dreams will make up the future that you decide to build.

The reality is, most love stories that make it to the big screen aren't the kind of ones that last in real life. Passion and intensity are important, but they're not everything. Falling in love, even in a once-in-a-lifetime way isn't enough to protect your relationship from hardship.

The relationship myths we grow up with often paint this image of a love that never stumbles or wavers. But those hard seasons we try to avoid aren't always a bad thing—they can lead to growth, greater intimacy, and a more authentic relationship. They're also not something you can run from forever.

Passion won't keep you together. Attraction doesn't help you deal with conflict. When life gets hard, and it will, relationships need intentional effort. Loving someone on purpose means choosing them even when they're driving you nuts.

Part of that whole "We all have baggage" thing is that we all grow up with predetermined ideas about relationships. Whether it's these myths or others, everyone has their own set of expectations and beliefs about what a relationship should look like. Whatever your relationship status is, it's worth questioning what these may be for you.

The process of identifying how your experiences and exposure to love has impacted the way you see it is a *huge step* towards healthier relationships, romantic or otherwise. Having high standards or expectations is not a bad thing—knowing what you want saves you *so* much time and emotional energy. But make sure that what you want is what *you* want—not just what you've been told to look for.

How to love on purpose

One of the weirdest things about starting a relationship is that everyone around you has an opinion. A lot of times, they feel entitled to share it with you. Of course, your inner circle and the people who know and love you the most are going to have some thoughts, as they should. But random strangers, distant friends, or loose acquaintances really have no business commenting.

It's all well-intentioned, of course. But the advice you're given from people who aren't close to you isn't always that valuable, and this is why:

Relationships aren't a one-size fits all. They're just not. While there are of course some non-negotiables to look for (respect, safety, love), there is no cookie cutter outline that defines what a healthy relationship looks like. What one person needs is going to be different from what another person needs.

Love Languages

Perhaps the best place to start when it comes to intentional love is identifying love languages.

"Love languages" are the ways in which we all give, receive, or experience love. They are: Words of

Affirmation, Quality Time, Receiving Gifts, Acts of Service, and Physical Touch (as characterized by Gary Chapman in his book <u>The Five Love Languages</u>[1]).

Everyone can connect to these ideas on some level, but we all have a hierarchy of what they mean to us. Some people feel most loved when someone else does something for them (Acts of Service), or if their significant other gives them a backrub (Physical Touch). This is one of the most important things you can know about a partner—how to love them in a way that they actually experience it.

You and your significant other may not have the same love languages. That's not a dealbreaker, or even necessarily a bad thing, but it does mean that you need to communicate with each other. Without intentionally trying to love someone in the way that they feel it, you can have couples *both* putting in tons of effort with little to no impact.

I'm a Words of Affirmation girl through and through (being a writer, you'd never know), and one of the greatest challenges in the early stages of my relationship was trying to communicate that to my boyfriend. We have one love language in common, but when it comes to Words, he doesn't *need* them in the same way that I do.

When we first started dating, I didn't know how to explain that I needed verbal affirmation in order to feel loved, and because of that, went through a lot of unnecessary anxiety and insecurity. To some extent, it doesn't matter what someone does for me—if they don't **tell me** that they're feeling a certain way, I will never assume it.

Write me a card and I'll cry from happiness. But clean my kitchen, get me a present, or hang out with me for a day—and I'll have no idea where we stand.

Love languages are astonishingly simple when you get used to them, but the information that they provide is invaluable. In the same way that knowing your own priorities enables you to act purposefully and effectively, knowing how to love your significant other is the key to doing it well.

Conflict

One of the most difficult parts of navigating healthy relationships is figuring out how to handle conflict. Because conflict **will** come. It's unavoidable, inevitable, and completely healthy. In fact, arguing with your partner may actually contribute to the health of your relationship.

Any long-term relationship (romantic or platonic) is going to reach a moment where you see things differently. This is not a bad thing. All it means is that you have two perspectives that clash, and as two separate people, it happens. You're not in a relationship with yourself, and your partner's opinions will not always mirror yours.

Consistent communication with your partner should lead to conflict semi-regularly, and that's actually a good sign.

The problem here comes in when couples or individuals lack the skills or experience to do conflict *well.*

The greatest misconception about conflict is that it always means fighting. It doesn't. Disagreeing is a normal part of life. 44% of married couples actually say that having conflict once a week allows them to keep their relationship both happy and productive.[2] It gives them a chance to express their thoughts, work through whatever's hanging over them, and move on.

It's working against each other that's destructive. Playing for two different teams. Trying to "win" an argument instead of finding a collaborative solution. Unwillingness to sacrifice or compromise at times.

If you're building a future together, you need to learn to be on the same team, even if you have different goals in the moment. Being in a relationship with someone that you love and trust won't be perfect, but you should be putting effort towards a mutual goal.

Try implementing these regular practices in order to make your communication more consistently effective:

Honesty:

This one seems obvious, but hear me out—Honesty is the *foundation* of healthy communication. If you want your partner to hear you, you have to be willing to speak up. Honesty isn't as simple as just not lying—it means actively choosing to tell the truth in your relationship.

If something is bothering you, bring it up. If your significant other hurt your feelings, crossed a line, or stepped on your toes, have a conversation. It's possible that they didn't know, and the longer you keep it in, the bigger an issue it will become.

Have you ever had one of those fights where halfway through the conversation you start to realize that they're not saying what you thought they were saying? When you're really struggling to hear each other or understand what the other person is saying, try repeating back to each other what you're hearing from them.

One of the most essential components to healthy communication in your relationships is being able to listen, not just talk. It's tough, but vital to hear your partner and work to understand what they're saying, no matter how you feel about it.

Take a step back:

A couple of months ago, I was at a bridal shower where a friend of mine asked the married women of the group to name the worst relationship advice they'd received. The unanimous agreement was that of all the cheesy slogans, one-liners, and "life hacks," the worst piece of advice they'd gotten was to never go to bed angry.

When you're working through something heavy, it's not always going to get resolved quickly. A 10 or 20-minute conversation doesn't solve a serious dilemma or difference.

Sometimes you have to go to bed angry. You need to take a walk, a pause, or a break from a conversation. Getting some space can help give you perspective, clarity, and allow you to come back prepared to communicate more effectively.

Communicate always

Communication is everything in relationships. Even when you're not mad, upset, or actually in conflict, being able to talk and connect effectively is essential.

Research has shown that poor communication is the number one reason why couples divorce—followed by an inability to resolve conflict.[3] Communicating is what keeps you on the same page. It's connecting with each other and respectfully dialoguing about what's happening in your lives and minds.

Conflict and communication are often intimidating things to approach in relationships, but they don't need to be.

John and Julie Gottman, psychologists and

co-founders of The Gottman Institute, have dedicated their lives, careers, and marriage to discovering what makes love really last. One of their most interesting discoveries was that there actually is a scientific ratio for how couples should fight.

The "magic ratio,"[4] as they call it, is a 5:1 ratio of positive interactions to negative ones. For every one negative interaction or fight, successful couples had five moments where they showed love to each other, had fun together, or built each other up.

These couples who fought or disagreed but remained engaged, intentional, and active in doing loving things for each other had much more successful relationships. They could be confident in knowing that their conflict was small in comparison to what their love did in their lives.

If you are lacking conflict in your long-term relationship, you are also lacking communication.

And both of those things are *musts* in creating a love that lasts.

These ideas—that conflict and red flags may not be the enemy, that strong relationships all look different, and that you actually get the freedom to *choose* who you want to spend your life with— run counter to so much of what love looks like in Hollywood or on social media.

It's not always Instagram-worthy. There are those moments—dancing in the kitchen, date nights, laughing hysterically over nothing, and they should far outweigh the negative ones—but there's going to be hard stuff too, and that's *normal*. Sometimes the most beautiful moments aren't the ones for anyone else to see. They're not what you'd expect. They can be "I'm sorry," "How can I help," or "Let's work through this together."

To be clear, though, love should always be more fun than it is hard. A healthy relationship takes *effort*, but it shouldn't feel like work. The love that you have for your person should empower and compel you to want to do these things together rather than weigh you down.

The intentional and purposeful action that you put into your career goals, habits, and personal growth needs also to be put into any relationship that matters.

Romantic or not, when you are spending regular time and emotional energy on someone, you are building something. Habits are forming, patterns are developing, and a potential future is taking shape. Whatever kind of love you want, it's not going to happen by accident. Intentional love is building a very specific foundation in order to create a strong future.

Intentionality in relationships is choosing a route

rather than just drifting until you end up somewhere. Trying to get there together.

Some would say that to love and love well is the ultimate purpose in life. Whether or not that made it onto your priority list, it's worth keeping in mind.

We were built for relationships, to do life with others, and doing it well matters.

A romantic partner is in no way a requirement or even a preference for living on purpose. Your relationship status has absolutely nothing to do with your worth, your potential, or your ability to live a full life.

But these things are important even in friendships. Knowing how to work through conflict, love your friends in ways that they feel loved, and communicate with your people can be completely transformative.

Whoever you have around you, if they matter to you, love them well. Invest in those relationships. Show up for them when they need you. Celebrate their wins, mourn their losses, and be present in all seasons.

To be honest, while intentionality is a game-changer in all areas of life, relationships are so central to who we are that without other people, it almost doesn't matter.

You were made to love and be loved. It is an innate

priority of your being. See it, value it, and pursue it with everything you have. Life is *so* much richer when shared with people you love.

CHAPTER TEN:
Like There's No Tomorrow

> "Twenty years from now you will be
> more disappointed by the things
> you didn't do than by the ones you
> did do. So throw off the bowlines.
> Sail away from the safe harbor.
> Catch the trade winds in your sails.
> Explore. Dream. Discover."[1]
>
> *H. Jackson Brown, Jr.*

So.

Here we are. The final chapter, and I still feel like I have so much to say. So many thoughts and experiences and musings bouncing around in my mind. I am aching to say everything and nothing all at once.

Instead, I want to leave you with three final thoughts. If you take anything away from this book, I hope it is these.

1. The best way to create a life you love is to become a person who knows how to love life.

Over the course of my life, I've been given many ideas about where to find happiness. Finding the right career, the right guy, the ideal circumstances. But to be honest, this runs contrary to my own lived experience, as well as all the research I've done both for this book and for my blog, articles for clients, and for fun.

Psychologically speaking, this doesn't make sense to me.

Instead of changing your world to be happy, it seems far more effective to *become* the kind of person who can find the best in life, even when it's mostly the worst.

By that, I do NOT mean toxic positivity—forcing yourself to fake happiness, ignoring your own emotions, pretending that real life doesn't suck sometimes. I mean being an *enthusiast*, looking for ways to brighten up dark spaces, "being the change."

We cannot simply demand that everything and everyone that we allow into our lives *serves* us. Not only is that illogical and unethical, it's wildly inconsistent with what's even possible.

Listen—if you're stuck in an unhealthy relationship, a toxic work environment, or a friendship that's harming you, by all means, either set boundaries or get out. But when you do, make sure that you are still capable of enjoying things that are good, or at least better.

The world as we know it will never be a place free of problems, suffering, or some kind of struggle. If you are trained to look for that, it's all you will see.

But when you learn to fall in love with life—with purpose, with people, with the things around you—everything gets better, and you'll find you can create a life you truly love right in the middle of the chaos.

2. The best way to grow is to embrace wrongness

I am the younger sister of an over-achieving, wildly talented, highly competitive brother. My childhood was basically a series of losing things—races, board games, unofficial debates around the dinner table. At the time, I hated it. It wasn't overly conducive to developing my confidence at the time. I was never even close to overpowering my brother in anything, but because of it, I got very comfortable with the idea of not being the best.

As an adult, I am endlessly, unbelievably grateful for this. Because I have learned that embracing wrongness (it's a word, I looked it up) has enabled me to grow like nothing else I've ever done.

Through the process of writing this book, I went through old blog posts, journal entries, and notes I had written years ago on these subjects. Some of them were helpful, some of them were funny, and some were just wrong.

But it was because I was once there that I have landed where I am.

The *best possible thing* that you can do for your growth is to embrace an ability to be wrong. Let go of the expectation that you're supposed to (or are capable of) get things right all the time.

This is particularly valuable when you are living a life on purpose. If you put too much pressure on yourself, if being wrong is your greatest fear, you will constantly be walking on eggshells and be unable to move forward or even see your decisions clearly.

Being wrong, especially about what you might want out of life, is the only way to really know what right is. There is some trial and error that you just can't avoid. I thought I would be a Film & TV Makeup Artist, and invested thousands on training to do just that. But without that wrongness, I wouldn't be in my dream job.

You are going to make mistakes and learn new things and it is going to be absolutely glorious. Embrace the process. Take your wrongness as an opportunity to practice accountability, learn, and redirect.

3. You cannot stay where you are.

It's impossible for me to know the details of your life at this exact moment. What I do know, however, is that it will not stay the same. Writing this in 2021, anyone who has lived through the last year and a half will know this to be true. Even if you choose to ignore any kind of purposeful living, your life will not and cannot stay the same.

There are moving pieces, people, and an entire world around you that are constantly changing and shifting. The things around you are not neutral. Whatever your goals in life are, they will not be arbitrarily achieved.

Regardless of what you do with the idea of intentional living, you are making choices about your life every day. To take one job is to not take another. To spend your evening reading is to not spend it watching TV. Investing in friendships, relationships, making sacrifices and choices and decisions and eliminating things that don't matter and embracing ones that do—each of these is playing a role in the shaping and making of your life and future.

Your choice is not between staying where you are and being something else. You and your life are going to shift no matter what. But when you accept an active, intentional role in your everyday life—even in the most mundane of tasks and choices - you have a much bigger role in deciding where you are going.

This is an opportunity. It's a responsibility. It's accepting the gift that you are given in each day and deciding to steward it well. *This* is what it means to live.

It is my sincere hope and goal that this book has inspired you to move. To act. Carpe diem, seize the day, and take ownership over your own life and time. Of the few guarantees we have in life, its shortness is one. Time isn't something to handle thoughtlessly or without care.

But with that said, sometimes this recognition leads to an unhelpful kind of action. Coming to terms with your own choices and mortality can create a mentality that's focused *too* heavily on action. Live like there's no tomorrow, go where no man has gone before, do everything and go everywhere and be loud and bold and big.

In theory, it's not necessarily a *bad* way of looking at things—but it's not really a healthy way either.

A full life doesn't necessarily mean a loud one. Good work doesn't have to be cutting edge. Living like there's no tomorrow is fine, but only if you are still living the way that you want to today.

Whatever point in life you're at, I hope you know that it's important. That even the most mundane of seasons are shaping you. That as long as you are showing up and committing to your every day, you are living on purpose.

What more could you hope for than a life filled with love, enthusiasm, conscious action, and good people?

You have one life, and you get to decide what it means to live it well. Whatever that is, I hope you go all in. I hope you are bold and brave and fearless in your pursuit. I hope you live every day on purpose, and with everything in you, refuse to settle for a lack of meaning.

You were created with purpose, with passion and gifts and potential that you have every ability to fulfill. Your story isn't over, and as the next chapter begins, open it simply with this one question:

What kind of life do you want to live?

A Note From the Author

My pursuit of a meaningful life began when I was 15 with the words of T.S. Eliot. I memorized and performed his poem, *The Hollow Men,* for a drama competition, and while I didn't win a medal, it did more for me than I could've imagined.

The poem depicts a haunting image of a world filled with empty people. Written as a reflection on European society post-WWI, its vivid imagery describes a death-like life. Meaningless, lacking—hollow.

The idea became a fear of mine, but rather than being a nightmare, it was a wake up call. A reminder that breathing does not equal living. At the time, I didn't know how to make sense of it, and had no idea how much this would come to shape my life, but I knew it was significant. I can no longer recite the whole piece, but the impact stuck with me.

Throughout this journey of purposeful living, I have grown, failed, loved, lost, laughed, cried, re-evaluated, and made mistakes more times than I can count. Intentionality has not kept me from being human, but rather elevated what it means in my life.

I have learned how to be a better friend, girlfriend, daughter, sister, and person. I have learned how to fall in love with life. How to do more than exist. How to see the little moments as more than little moments.

I've witnessed this change in the life of others, too, and I know how much it can do.

Ernest Hemingway is quoted as saying *"In order to write about life first you must live it*." And those words used to haunt me—because as I live, I learn, and to publish anything in a permanent manner, where I cannot simply add a sentence and chapter anytime I learn something new is daunting. How would I know when I'd lived enough to write?

This was and has been a genuine fear of mine. But in writing this book, I have been reminded of what it really *is* to learn and live and become. I don't think I'll ever reach a point where I feel I've lived "enough" to write. But I discovered quickly in the process that where I thought I would struggle to pull from life experience, I instead struggled to stop the words from pouring out of me.

Writing this book was the hardest and scariest thing I've ever done. The fearful part of me didn't want to write it at all—

But how could I not?

After experiencing such a gift in this way of life, to keep it to myself is unthinkable. And so, while releasing this book into the world is both unbelievably thrilling and completely terrifying, I am humbly and optimistically hopeful that what I know to be life-changing will do the same for you as it has for me.

This book is not the end for either of us. We will keep living and keep learning. I'm sure that one day I'll look back and want to add a sentence or a chapter or an essay, but perhaps I'll save it for another book. Right now, all I have left to say is thank you. For reading, for trusting me. Your time is a gift I do not take lightly. Whatever you're walking away with, I hope it's enriching and fulfilling.

I truly cannot put into words how much this project has meant to me. As I continue to grow, I will continue to write, but I will never have another first book, and perhaps none so personally meaningful.

I look forward to this journey with you and continually discovering what it means to live life on purpose.

Acknowledgments

The power of community is no joke. The amount of love and support that has been poured into this book from day one brings me to my knees, and while "Thank you" feels too small and insignificant a term to honestly express the gratitude I feel to the people who have partnered with me on this, it's all I have.

To Zach—the first person I told about this project, my biggest cheerleader, best friend, and love. You make me better.

To my lifelong editor, Mom, this project would not be here without you, and neither would I. Thank you for your time, patience, persistence, and love.

Rees, the brilliant mind behind the cover design of this book—from the moment we connected, you caught the vision of the project and brought so much talent and skill. You captured the feel, message, and meaning of this book so beautifully. Thank you.

Katie, from the moment we met, I felt that we were

put into each other's lives for a reason. Every season we have gone through together has proven this correct. Your knowledge, support, and friendship means more to me than I could put into words.

Dad and Micah, you both inspire me everyday. Thank you for believing in me and in my writing even when I didn't.

To every friend, family member, and piece of my community—thank you a thousand times over.

Finally, to you, the reader—thank you for being here, for taking this step, and for daring to dream of a life that you love.

References

Introduction

1. Solan, M. (2021, November 1). *Health and happiness go hand in hand*. Harvard Health. https://www.health.harvard.edu/mind-and-mood/health-and-happiness-go-hand-in-hand

Chapter Two

1. *'All-or-Nothing' Thinking More Common in People with Anxiety, Depression, and Suicidal Ideation – Association for Psychological Science – APS*. (n.d.). Retrieved November 27, 2021, from https://www.psychologicalscience.org/publications/observer/obsonline/all-or-nothing-thinking-more-common-in-people-with-anxiety-depression-and-suicidal-ideation.html

2. Haden, J. (2018, June 4). *New Research Reveals What People Regret Most of All: 5 Ways to Make Sure You Never Do*. Inc.Com. https://www.inc.com/jeff-haden/new-research-reveals-what-people-regret-most-of-all-5-ways-to-make-sure-you-never-do.html

3. *The Truth About the Law of Attraction | Psychology Today Canada*. (n.d.). Retrieved November 27, 2021, from https://www.psychologytoday.com/ca/blog/the-blame-game/201609/the-truth-about-the-law-attraction

Chapter Three

1. *Oxford Languages and Google—English | Oxford Languages*. (n.d.). Retrieved November 27, 2021, from https://languages.oup.com/google-dictionary-en/

2. *Positive thinking: Reduce stress by eliminating negative self-talk—Mayo Clinic*. (n.d.). Retrieved November 27, 2021, from https://www.mayoclinic.org/healthy-lifestyle/stress-management/in-depth/positive-thinking/art-20043950

3. Post, S. G. (2005). Altuism, happiness, and health: It's good to be good. *International Journal of Behavioral Medicine, 12*(2), 66–77. https://doi.org/10.1207/s15327558ijbm1202_4

4. *Classics in the History of Psychology—Yerkes & Dodson (1908)*. (n.d.). Retrieved November 27, 2021, from http://psychclassics.yorku.ca/Yerkes/Law/

5. *Aren't sure? Brain is primed for learning*. (2018, July 19). YaleNews. https://news.yale.edu/2018/07/19/arent-sure-brain-primed-learning

Chapter Four

1. Clear, J. (2018). *Atomic habits: Tiny changes, remarkable results: an easy & proven way to build good habits & break bad ones*. Avery, an imprint of Penguin Random House.

2. Tennant, A. (1995, November 17). *It Takes Two*. Warner Bros.

3. *Most People Fail to Achieve Their New Year's Resolution. For Success, Choose a Word of the Year Instead | Inc.com*. (n.d.). Retrieved November 27, 2021, from https://www.inc.com/marla-tabaka/why-set-yourself-up-for-failure-ditch-new-years-resolution-do-this-instead.html

4. *Why 3% of Harvard MBAs Make Ten Times as Much as the Other 97% Combined | Sid Savara*. (n.d.). Retrieved November 27, 2021, from https://sidsavara.com/why-3-of-harvard-mbas-make-ten-times-as-much-as-the-other-97-combined/

Chapter Five

1. *It's not you. Phones are designed to be addicting. - YouTube*. (n.d.). Retrieved November 27, 2021, from https://www.youtube.com/watch?v=NUMa0QkPzns

2. Clear, J. (2018). *Atomic habits: Tiny changes, remarkable results: an easy & proven way to build good habits & break bad ones*. Avery, an imprint of Penguin Random House.

3. *The Holy Bible (English Standard Version).* (n.d.).

4. Durant, W. (1953). *The Story of Philosophy: The Lives and Opinions of the Greater Philosophers.* Washington Square Pr.

5. Duhigg, C. (2014). *The power of habit: Why we do what we do in life and business.*

6. Institute, D. N. (2019, July 22). *22 Facts About the Brain | World Brain Day.* DENT Neurologic Institute. https://www.dentinstitute.com/posts/lifestyle-tips/22-facts-about-the-brain-world-brain-day/

7. *Does Thinking Burn Calories? Here's What the Science Says | Time.* (n.d.). Retrieved November 27, 2021, from https://time.com/5400025/does-thinking-burn-calories/

8. *Why Monday is the Best Day for Setting New Goals.* (n.d.). Association for Psychological Science - APS. Retrieved November 27, 2021, from https://www.psychologicalscience.org/news/minds-business/why-monday-is-the-best-day-for-setting-new-goals.html

9. Fogg, B. J. (2019). *Tiny habits: The small changes that change everything.* Houghton Mifflin Harcourt.

Chapter Six

1. Eurich, T. (2018). *Insight: The surprising truth about how others see us, how we see ourselves, and why the answers matter more*

than we think (First trade paperback edition). Currency.

2. *Https://www.enneagraminstitute.com/*. (n.d.).

Chapter Seven

1. *This Is What 'Self-Care' REALLY Means, Because It's Not All Salt Baths And Chocolate Cake | Thought Catalog*. (n.d.). Retrieved November 27, 2021, from https://thought-catalog.com/brianna-wiest/2017/11/this-is-what-self-care-really-means-because-its-not-all-salt-baths-and-chocolate-cake/

Chapter Eight

1. Writer, L. M. H. S. (2017, April 11). Over nearly 80 years, Harvard study has been showing how to live a healthy and happy life. *Harvard Gazette*. https://news.harvard.edu/gazette/story/2017/04/over-nearly-80-years-harvard-study-has-been-showing-how-to-live-a-healthy-and-happy-life/

2. Waldinger, R. (1450889841). *What makes a good life? Lessons from the longest study on happiness*. https://www.ted.com/talks/robert_waldinger_what_makes_a_good_life_lessons_from_the_longest_study_on_happiness

3. Chartrand, T. L., & Bargh, J. A. (1999). The chameleon effect: The perception–behavior link and social interaction. *Journal of Personality and Social Psychology*, *76*(6), 893–910. https://doi.org/10.1037/0022-3514.76.6.893

4. Brown, B. (2015). *Daring greatly: How the courage to be vulnerable transforms the way we live, love, parent, and lead* (First trade paperback printing). Avery.

Chapter Nine

1. Chapman, G. D. (2015). *The 5 love languages*. Northfield Pub.

2. *Scientists Claim That Couples Who Fight a Lot Really Love Each Other*. (2018, December 8). Bright Side — Inspiration. Creativity. Wonder. https://brightside.me/inspiration-relationships/ scientists-claim-that-couples-who-fight-a-lot-really-love-each-other-658710/

3. *Poor Communication Is The #1 Reason Couples Split Up: Survey | HuffPost Life*. (n.d.). Retrieved November 27, 2021, from https://www.huffpost.com/entry/ divorce-causes-_n_4304466

4. *The Magic Relationship Ratio, According to Science*. (2017, October 4). The Gottman Institute. https://www.gottman.com/blog/ the-magic-relationship-ratio-according-science/

Resource Page

Over the last several years, I've been heavily impacted by countless authors, speakers, educators, and more. These leaders have taught me, directly or otherwise, so much about living on purpose. I could not possibly list every individual who has impacted me, but I do want to share some of the resources that have made the greatest difference in my life.

These books, podcasts, and videos are the ones that have stuck with me in a different way. Most of my friends can attest to the fact that I reference them frequently, and accredit a lot of my own growth here.

Books

1. **Atomic Habits by James Clear** - If you're not sure where to go from here, I would recommend starting with Atomic Habits. It's a closer look at the role habits play in our lives, and is chock-full of easy to understand psychology and principles that will transform the routines in your life.

2. **Essentialism by Greg McKeown** - Essentialism is all about cultivating "less but better" in your life. It expands on the principle of making room for what matters by cutting out what doesn't. I *highly* recommend this book, and personally quite enjoyed the audiobook format.

3. **The Ruthless Elimination of Hurry by John Mark Comer** - John Mark Comer's books and teachings have impacted me personally in more ways than I can count. This book is *so* rich, especially for Christians. If you feel caught up in the hustle, worn out, or stuck, read this book.

4. **Garden City by John Mark Comer**

5. **Crucial Conversations by Kerry Patterson, Joseph Grenny, Al Switzler, and Ron McMillan** - The principles in this book are invaluable for approaching conflict, hard conversations, or tough moments with anyone in your life.

6. **Boundaries by Henry Cloud and John Townsend**

7. **The Mountain is You by Brianna Wiest** - Although I haven't actually read this book yet, I'm a big fan of Brianna Wiest. This book tackles self-sabotage and the ways in which we so often make things harder for ourselves.

8. **Daring Greatly by Brené Brown**

Videos

9. 3 psychological tricks to help you save money | The Way We Work, a TED series https://www.youtube.com/watch?v=DOisAG9yoNk&t=212s

10. Robert Waldinger: What makes a good life? Lessons from the longest study on happiness | TED https://www.youtube.com/watch?v=8KkKuTCFvzI

11. The Science of Habits | Marco Badwal https://www.youtube.com/watch?v=FSZyzhi8C9o&t=842s

About the Author

Anika Green was born in Madison, Wisconsin, but grew up and currently resides in British Columbia, Canada (although the Packers will always be #1). She is a passionate writer, encourager, and enthusiast of life and intentionality. Her blog, *outofthehabit.com* is visited by thousands of monthly readers and filled with resources, articles, and tools to purposefully create a life you love. Out of the Habit is her first full-length publication.

Instagram @anikajgreen
outofthehabit.com
Anikajgreen.com
Please send any inquiries to
anika@outofthehabit.com.
Headshot taken by Cecilia Reusch

Made in the USA
Middletown, DE
18 January 2022

59079696R00139